EIGHTEENTH CENTURY PIETY

EIGHTEENTH CENTURY PIETY

BY

W. K. LOWTHER CLARKE

LONDON

SOCIETY FOR PROMOTING
CHRISTIAN KNOWLEDGE

NEW YORK: THE MACMILLAN COMPANY

First published 1944
Reprinted 1945

MADE IN GREAT BRITAIN

PREFACE

THE purpose of this book is to contribute to the history of the S.P.C.K., first by summarising the books published by the Society in the eighteenth century; secondly by telling the story of a great and good man, Henry Newman, Secretary from 1708 to 1743. I am indebted to the authorities of the Society for leave to use his unpublished letters. The rest of the book has been written at intervals during the last thirty years, and though mainly concerned with the eighteenth century sometimes goes outside it. These minor exercises are best described as recreations.

The title, *Eighteenth Century Piety*, was chosen with some misgivings. It may suggest a more devotional treatment than will be actually found. But I wanted to keep the word " piety ".

> The Child is father of the Man ;
> And I could wish my days to be
> Bound each to each by natural piety.

This applies to the successive generations of the Church of England. In spite of many good books which have helped to reverse the nineteenth century's depreciation of its predecessor (among which I may mention Miss M. G. Jones, *The Charity School Movement*, Dr. N. Sykes' *Church and State in XVIII Century England* and *Edmund Gibson*, Canon Smyth's *Simeon and Church Order*, and Dr. Wickham Legg's *English Church Life*), there is still room for further studies inspired by " natural piety ". *Pietas* signifies filial affection, and this is exactly what I feel towards the persons here studied. To live with William Jones, Henry Newman, William Stevens, and Mrs. Trimmer is to love them.

Of these essays, first sketches of I, IV(*b*), (*g*), and VII appeared in the *Church Quarterly Review*; V, VIII, X (in a shorter form), XII, XIV, XV, XVI, and XVIII were printed in *Theology*; VI was first published in the *English Church Review*; and XVII in the *Teaching Church Review*. Canon Jenkins has given valuable help in providing me with the names of authors of certain anonymous works in I.

37230

v

CONTENTS

LIST OF ILLUSTRATIONS

(See end of book)

I

PASTORALIA

The conventional verdict on the Church of England of the eighteenth century is still so widely accepted that another attempt at reconsideration is justified. Lytton Strachey's brilliant essay on "Cardinal Manning" in *Eminent Victorians* repeats it—"for many generations the Church of England had slept the sleep of the . . . comfortable". H. O. Wakeman in his widely read *History of the Church of England* makes these remarks: "As the bells rang out in 1714 to welcome the accession of George I, they sounded the death-knell of her [the Church of England's] high ideals and vigorous life for more than a century. . . . Quiet and satisfaction reigned supreme. . . . The practice of daily service in town churches was given up. . . . If they [the clergy] had thought out their theological position they must have classed themselves almost to a man as Low Churchmen." I do not want to dispute these judgments, for which abundant evidence can be produced. Nor do I aim at a balanced appraisement of all the facts. All I propose to do is to pursue one line of inquiry, into the contents of the books published by the S.P.C.K. Anticipating my results, I can say with certainty that there is evidence leading to different conclusions and that the one thing we shall not find is any spirit of complacency.

I propose, then, to describe English Church life in the eighteenth century as it appears to one who reads the books and pamphlets put out by the S.P.C.K. Although so much has been written on the subject, this source has never been used, so far as I know. It is of peculiar importance. The Society was under episcopal patronage, and through its correspondents in touch with priests and laymen all over the country. As a Church Publishing Society it stood alone. Its usual method was to make a selection of what had been already published, and to buy large quantities for distribution to members and for sale to the public. (Books were sold to the members at the cost of the quires and pamphlets at half the actual cost.) Only rarely did it accept manuscripts offered in the ordinary way. Once a book was on the list it stayed there for many years, even for generations, sometimes revised at its successive editions, more often remaining unchanged. For example, Bishop Beveridge's *Sermon on the Common Prayer*, first published in 1681, was reprinted in 1799 in a thirty-eighth edition. The Rev. Francis Fox, Vicar of

St. Mary's, Reading, joined the S.P.C.K. at the beginning of the eighteenth century. His *Duty of Public Worship Proved* reached its ninth edition in 1771. A Funeral Sermon on the death of the Earl of Rochester in 1680 was still being reprinted as late as 1798, to give away at funerals. We may admit an excess of conservatism in the Committee, but may none the less conclude that throughout the century there was general agreement as to the literature needs of the Church. Society was static throughout the period, at least in comparison with our standards of rapid change. Also we may fairly suppose that the books selected for such long-continued and widespread use were typical, and that from their statements and implications we may draw valid conclusions as to actual conditions as well as ideals.

Dr. Sykes tells the story of Bishop Gibson's close association with the Society, both in the administration of Charity Schools and in the provision of pastoral literature. " This important function [of publishing educative literature] had now been controlled almost to monopoly by the Society for Promoting Christian Knowledge, which thus became the chief and more permanent influence in stemming the tide of irreligion and immorality." So says Dr. Sykes, who pays a too generous tribute to " the perennial vigour of that Society ". [1]

The Society's literature during the century is uniformly High Church, in the contemporary sense of the word. The passages which I shall select are fairly representative of the whole, and there is nothing to contradict them. Bishop Horsley, of St. David's, in 1790, rebukes his clergy's fear of being called High Churchmen.[2]

> To be a High-Church-Man, in the only sense which the word can be allowed to bear, as applicable to any in the present day ; God forbid, that this should ever cease to be my public pretension, my pride, my glory ! To be a High-Church-Man in the true import of the word in the English language, God forbid, that ever I should deserve the imputation !

He explains that the traditional sense is one who claims the powers, honours and emoluments which are enjoyed under an establishment ; but by this time it has come to mean one who recognizes the spiritual authority of the priesthood. " My reverend brethren, we must be content to be High-Church-Men according to this usage of the word, or we cannot at all be Churchmen." [3]

---

[1] *Edmund Gibson*, pp. 197–8.
[2] The Charge, like all the other books mentioned in this chapter, was published by the S.P.C.K.
[3] Throughout this book I have disregarded the excessive capitalization

CHURCHMANSHIP

Robert Nelson, the non-juror, who joined the S.P.C.K. in 1699, often took the chair at its meetings. His books were distributed from the first and nearly all later manuals recommended them for fuller information. Bishop Ken's and Bishop Wilson's works were equally popular. Nelson's rule of life in *The Nature and Wisdom of True Devotion* (new edition 1827) is very searching. In the morning, after private prayer, Bible-reading, and a quarter of an hour spent on a good book, follow family prayers, and then comes the daily service in church, if possible. The day's work is to be dedicated to God and sanctified by frequent ejaculatory prayer. At night come family prayers again, and as part of private devotions careful self-examination. Bishop Ken's hymns are to be learned by heart and said on going to sleep, and at midnight if you are awake. Fast days are to be kept, even to the extent of sometimes taking no food until the evening. One virtue is to be cultivated on each day of the week : on Sunday, the love of God ; Monday, the love of our neighbour ; Tuesday, humility ; Wednesday, patience ; Thursday, improvement of our talents ; Friday, mortification ; Saturday, chastity. The meditation recommended is of the intellectual kind, and there is nothing in the nature of contemplative prayer.

Nelson and Ken, although non-jurors, set the tone of S.P.C.K. Churchmanship. A less familiar book than theirs is Archbishop Wake's (d. 1737) *The Principles of the Christian Religion Explained, in a Brief Commentary on the Church Catechism*,[1] the merits of which are outstanding. No such lucid, concise, and complete book on the Catechism is in common use today. Of the Catholic Church he says : "We profess not our faith of any one particular Church ; which may cease ; and fail, (such as the Church of England, or Church of Rome). . . ." A particular Church may not be called "the Catholic Church". "But a Catholic Church, a particular Church may be called ; and such ours is." The Church of England is a true part of the Catholic Church, "inasmuch as it professes the true Catholic faith, delivered in the Holy Scriptures, and drawn up in the creeds of the Church". "The Communion of Saints" in the original denotes "either holy persons or holy things". Our com-

---

of the initial letters of nouns in transcribing passages, because the usage varies and by the end of the period becomes the same as today's ; frequently I have been able to use only the later editions, in which the change has been made. I have preserved the punctuation.

[1] Written when he was Bishop of Lincoln.

munion is also with the departed. It is probable that they pray for us. Ministers " are called in to the assistance of sick or scrupulous persons " ; in pronouncing absolution " they only declare the sentence of God ; which, if a sinner be truly penitent, God will infallibly make good ". But absolution is declarative, not judicial.

CHURCH SERVICES

Churchgoing on Sunday was represented primarily as a duty, there was no thought of making services " attractive". Manuals to explain the service, implying a very high level of devotion, were circulated. Preparation at home is taught (for Mattins, as we teach preparation for Holy Communion), and prayers are provided for use while walking to church with your family, on entering the church-yard, at the church door, etc. (*The Pious Parishioner*). This book remarks : " The age we live in (thanks be to God) abounds with pious books ; and it is to be hoped the world is bettered by them." Very elementary advice is given—to kneel for prayer, to stand for the psalms and hymns. It was customary for those who could read to say the prayers with the minister. They are taught that they must not do this audibly, and not at all in the case of the Absolution. The Psalms and Canticles, according to Mrs. Trimmer at the end of the century, are sung in Cathedrals, " but in churches generally they are read". *The Excellent Use of Psalmody*,[1] from directions given by Bishop Gibson in 1724, was the popular guide. The tunes are to be plain, out-of-the-way and ridiculous ones being avoided. " Guard against the indecencies that parish-clerks who are not duly qualified, always bring into the public worship."

A French observer reported that the Sunday morning service lasted an hour and a half.[2] The afternoon service was shorter. Owing to pluralism one service on Sunday was common in country parishes. The omission of a sermon in the afternoon was frequent and people would go to a distant church for the sermon when there was only catechizing in their own church.

The sermon was the climax of the service in spite of the manuals of devotion. The seventeenth century splendour of diction and emotion had passed away, superseded by a new clarity and simplicity of style.[3] The whitewash on the walls of the church was put there

---

[1] Psalmody meant the metrical psalms, or the few other hymns sung at the time.

[2] The Marquis de la Rochefoucauld. See N. Sykes, *Church and State in the Eighteenth Century.*

[3] Sykes, p. 257. W. Fraser Mitchell's *English Pulpit Oratory* is a mine of information.

for the sake of cleanliness and economy, but was felt to be symbolical of the age of reason (" God is light "), a fitting reaction from the mystery of Gothic. The themes of the sermon were consonant with the new clarity and were chiefly the Fatherhood of God and the duty of benevolence in man.[1]

A story is told of a man who used to keep his bank-notes in Tillotson's Sermons, thus getting a double safeguard : it was unlikely, he explained, that a burglar would care for sermons ; and, if he did, unlikely that he would appreciate Tillotson's. But in our period they were often read and in any case imitated. Bishop Burnet's opinion, in his *Pastoral Care*, is typical : " the noblest body of Sermons that, I hope I may be allowed to say, this nation, or the world, ever saw ".[2] *An Address to the People Called Methodists*, after describing their excesses, says : " When they had presumed to go these lengths, it is no wonder they should take the liberty to condemn those excellent writings, *The Whole Duty of Man* and Archbishop Tillotson's works."

The primary charge to his clergy of Archbishop Hort (Tuam) in 1742 was adopted by the S.P.C.K. and republished as late as 1819. It urged a plain and easy style, laying aside metaphysical subtleties, attacked " that *subsaltory* way of delivery, that rises like a storm in one part of the period and presently sinks into a dead calm that will scarce reach the ear ", and pleaded for a revival of " that almost antiquated exercise of expounding the Holy Scripture to your congregation ". Archdeacon Paley, towards the end of the century, said, if you cannot compose a sermon every week, at least do so once a month. Written sermons were the ordinary custom. " Reading [sermons] is peculiar to this nation, and is endured in no other," says Bishop Burnet. According to Mrs. Trimmer, the clergyman prefaced the sermon with a prayer, followed by " Our Father ".

The middle class, as might be expected, were the most regular in church attendance. A tract of about 1830, *Tracts on Practical Subjects addressed to the Working Classes*, No. V, says : " Within the last half century the Sunday has been much more strictly observed by the upper and middle classes than formerly ", adding that few of the working classes go to church. Sunday trading, which is probably unavoidable, is one reason. (" You would willingly go

[1] Sykes, p. 233.
[2] A very useful exercise for the student would be the reconstruction of the minds of successive generations from the sermons to which they listened with most pleasure.

to church, but you make a good deal of money in the shop on Sundays, and you cannot give that up ", says No. I of the series.) Mr. Fox (*The Duty of Public Worship Proved*, 9th ed. 1771) adds another, that the week-end is the time generally chosen for a dose.

As regards Holy-days, Bishop Porteous (d. 1809) comments on the great revival in the observance of Good Friday. Mrs. Trimmer says that " Christmas-day, and the eleven days following, are considered holidays ". The Great Week, or Holy Week, " is now called Passion Week ". Monday and Tuesday in Easter and Whitsun Weeks are often spent in riot and drunkenness. King Charles I's death is reckoned as a national sin and he is treated as a saint in the Calendar ; Oak-apple day is observed on May 29th.[1]

Dr. Sykes says [2] that daily prayers were increasingly neglected during the century, the indifference being due largely to the absence of a sermon. In 1743 the Diocese of York had twenty-four churches with daily prayer, eighty with service on Wednesdays and Fridays and Holy-days ; and out of 836 parishes only 253 had some kind of daily service more or less regularly.[3]

Our books seem to show that the Daily Office was better attended than it is today. In 1794 a new edition was brought out of *An Essay on the Service of the Church of England considered as a Daily Service, with a view of reviving a more general and constant Attendance upon it*, by William Best, D.D. The book had been in circulation for more than fifty years, and was now revised to make it suit the whole Church. " A Personage " (presumably the King) attends regularly —what an example to all of us ! The book is addressed especially to London, Westminster, and market towns. The author laments that " so few, even of the serious and well-disposed part of them, ever attend upon it ", though it need not take more than half an hour. Country towns are an example to great cities.

" In market and other populous towns such a congregation is usually to be met with, two days of the week at least, as bears some proportion to the number of inhabitants." The Daily Office is of course said in Cathedrals and Bishops' palaces, but not any longer in noblemen's houses. Alas ! many town churches are shut on week days, which is the main cause of the increase of private baptisms. In those which are open the worshippers have fallen to two or three,

---

[1] When I was a boy in York bands of children used to go round to people's houses, asking money and chanting " Twenty-ninth of May, Oak-apple day, If you don't give us a holiday, We'll all run away ".
[2] *Church and State*, p. 247.
[3] Sykes, *Edmund Gibson*, p. 221.

but these are very devout, and frequent in their attendance at Holy Communion. After this lament we are surprised to read : " Blessed be God for the opportunities that are reached out in so many places of enjoying the celebration of the daily service; especially the evening, at an hour when the laborious duties of the day may be supposed to be at an end." This seems to show that the writer has been exaggerating somewhat the extent of the falling off. The parochial clergy, he concludes, must set an example by repairing, with their families, to church at least on Wednesdays, Fridays, fasts and festivals. If there is no congregation at their own church, then they must go to a neighbouring church; they cannot be exonerated from the observance of the rubric. This demand is significant. It implies that a priest did not say his office in church alone, or even with no congregation other than his own family, but that a larger attendance was normal.

The Christian Monitor (1774 ed.), a popular devotional book throughout the century, says : " See that you duly resort to your parish churches, and that not only on holidays, but on the weekdays, when you have opportunity and leisure."

An Account of the Workhouses (1732) refers to daily service in many parts of England. The inmates at St. Andrew's, Holborn, attend twice each week day. At Bedford " the oldest people creep out to church upon prayer days ". At Maidstone the old people go to church every day, children and those of working age on Wednesday and Friday. At Finedon, in Northamptonshire, the twenty girls in the workhouse go every day. It is unlikely that the illiterate poor formed the only congregation. The clergy are frequently mentioned as visiting the workhouses, and the master or mistress reads prayers every day. The authorities would hardly have made a rule of church-going in addition, if public opinion had not supported them, and if the practice of attending the Daily Office had not been widespread in the higher ranks of society.

THE SACRAMENTS

(a) Baptism

This is everywhere presupposed, there was no need to justify it. Archbishop Wake answers the question " How can any one make promises for another ? " very lucidly. " Upon a supposition of charity : that as children are born of Christian parents, and under a security of being bred up to a sense and knowledge of their

duty in this particular, and of the infinite obligations that lie upon
them to fulfil it ; so they will take care (by God's help) so to order
both their faith and manners, as their interest as well as duty
requires them to do." If they do not fulfil the promise, "in that
case the covenant made on their behalf will be void". "Would it
not be more reasonable to tarry till persons are grown up, and so
in a condition to make the covenant themselves, before they were
permitted to be baptized?" "We are not to consider what we
think best, but what God has directed us to do." Our children
are as capable of entering into the covenant as the Jews' children
were at eight days.

The Christian Monitor, which seems to suppose that baptisms
took place during the ordinary service, urges attendance at them
as frequently as possible, to remind us of our own initiation. *A
Serious Address to Godfathers and Godmothers* (new ed. 1804) sums
up their duties, which are to see that the children attend catechizing,
and go forward to Confirmation ; to step into the place of the
parents if they die or fail to attend to the spiritual care of the children ;
to see that they are taught to read, and to give them good books ;
and, if they go into service, to help them to places in godly families.

(b) Catechizing

The evidence as to this is conflicting. Wake says that the introduction of a second sermon in the afternoon " has almost quite
thrown out the much better, and more profitable, exercise of
catechising ". In 1695 the Metropolitan directed his suffragans to
recommend to their clergy " since they must preach . . . to preach
in the afternoon upon catechetical heads ". Archbishop Secker in
1741 said that in few places is catechizing omitted ; but in many
churches it is confined to Lent.[1] Archbishop Synge's (Tuam)
charge to his clergy (1742) must have been considered suitable for
English conditions, since it was adopted by the S.P.C.K. He says
that catechizing is becoming unpopular because it prolongs the
service by half an hour. The Rev. Sir James Stonhouse, in *The
Religious Instruction of Children Recommended*, reports that the
neglect is due to the carelessness of parents and to the excessive
crowding of the aisles, which leaves no room for the children.
" There have been, and still are some in the exalted stations of life,
who have made a conscience of having their children publicly
catechized in the church, which is a very laudable example." The

[1] Sykes, *Church and State*, pp. 244-5.

minister should catechize in the vestry, or in the church before or after the service. As late as 1794 *A Present for Servants* (11th ed.) urges the practice, which so far as young men and women are concerned is falling into desuetude. " I know the usual plea is, that you are ashamed to answer, especially before the congregation." Rather than forgo it, they should come privately by night, like Nicodemus. It is valuable evidence of earnest pastoral care that so widely circulated a manual can assume the willingness of the clergy to give private instruction in the parsonage house.

(c) Confirmation

Little remains to be added to Canon Ollard's exhaustive essay on the post-Reformation period in *Confirmation : or the Laying on of Hands*, Vol. I. He concludes that candidates, at least of the educated classes, prepared themselves. This is probably right. In that individualistic age it was the obvious course for *catechized young people*. They knew the faith of the Church, and needed devotional preparation, which had to be their own work. Throughout the century the Society circulated *Pastoral Advice to Young Persons, in order to their being Confirmed by the Bishop* (9th ed. 1759) and *Instructions for those that come to be Confirmed* (22nd ed. 1758) both anonymous, by Josiah Woodward. Preparation, says the latter, consists of self-examination, confession to God, serious resolutions, and fasting. In Confirmation " God vouchsafes to communicate supernatural strength to overcome their spiritual enemies, and enables them to perform what they undertake ". *Pastoral Advice* tells " young men and women " to study the Catechism and the Preface to *The Whole Duty of Man*, and to resort to the minister, who will advise and assist and " ought to be satisfied of your fitness for Confirmation " before presenting you. The Archbishop's directions to the parochial clergy are given. They include the following : (1) find out who are not baptized ; (2) examine and instruct them ; (3) especially in the doctrine of Baptism ; (4) permit none to come twice ; (5) present none under fourteen, " unless they are greater proficients in Christian knowledge and piety, than children ordinarily are at those ages " ; (6) make a list with ages ; (11) prepare the confirmed for Holy Communion.

By the end of the century the usual age had become sixteen. Earlier Bishop Burnet had said the children must understand what they do, and Robert Nelson in *Instructions for those that come to be Confirmed* that there was no fixed age.

B

Besides the two manuals mentioned above there are a number of others, in all of which careful instructions are given on self-examination and repentance, with devotions for use on the actual day. It was a common practice to give candidates a pamphlet containing the Prayer Book service with appropriate prayers. Mrs. Trimmer says that the minister calls on the children to prepare themselves for examination, gives them little books, and catechizes them from time to time. The method had changed little since the days of Bishop Wilson, who wrote in *The Principles and Duties of Churchmanship* : " Having notice to prepare myself for Confirmation, I beg your assistance, that I may know what I am going about ", and was more like that of today than is generally believed. After Confirmation the candidates were given further little books to help them in preparation for Communion. Of the teaching in both sets of manuals we may say that it is austere, theologically sound, not lightened by illustrative matter, and altogether of a kind which would be considered too dry and difficult for young people today. There is no indication that easier ways were ever contemplated. Some clergy were careless and failed to live up the pastoral ideal set before them ; but it remained the ideal.

Dr. Sykes has done great service by showing the physical difficulties which prevented elderly bishops from getting about their large dioceses to confirm. Archbishop Wake [1] significantly says : " If it be possible, they should endeavour to be confirmed, and thereby fully take upon themselves the first sacrament, before they proceed to the participation of the second." It is clear from this that considerable use was made of the rubric about being " ready and desirous to be confirmed ".

To conclude : the clergy would have been surprised to learn that they would be deemed by posterity not to have prepared candidates, for Confirmation ; but preparation meant ascertaining that the Catechism was known and understood, and helping candidates to prepare themselves devotionally. A body of catechized young people was presupposed. Preparation for Holy Communion followed the ceremony.

(d) Holy Communion

Many writers urge " frequent " Communion. Thus Archbishop Tillotson (d. 1694) wrote *A Persuasive to Frequent Communion*

[1] Who adds a catechetical chapter on Confirmation to his book on the Catechism.

(10th ed. 1818). Bishop Gibson (d. 1748) advocated it in *The Sacrament of the Lord's Supper Explained*. " A Layman ", about 1804, wrote *An Earnest Exhortation to a Frequent Reception of the Holy Sacrament* ; [1] of this booklet 21,000 copies were sold in ten years. What did these writers mean by " frequent " ?

Dr. Sykes gives these figures. In York diocese, in 1743, of 836 churches seventy-two had monthly celebrations, 363 quarterly, 208 fell below that level, and 193 varied from four to six Sacrament Days in the year. In Bangor diocese, in 1749, Holy Communion was celebrated in most parishes monthly. Four times a year was the practice in Parson Woodforde's parishes. In London most churches had monthly celebrations, eleven in 1728 had weekly.[2]

Our documents agree that the Sacrament was much neglected in country parishes, but London set a good example. Early Communion is attested by *A Friendly Call to the Holy Communion* (1746) at The Chapel Royal, Whitehall Chapel, St. Martin-in-the-Fields, St. Anne's Aldersgate, St. Michael's Crooked Lane, St. Mary-le-Bow, and St. Dunstan-in-the-West ; at the last two also on Holy-days. Dr. Best's *Essay on the Service of the Church of England*, before 1770, says : " Our Church requireth, or at least supposeth, it to be administered every Lord's Day, and every Holiday throughout the year ". James Bonnell, whose Life was a favourite devotional book from 1702, the date of publication, till 1821 (7th ed.), communicated weekly in Dublin. Bishop Beveridge's (d. 1704) sermon on the subject, popular throughout the century, longs for a weekly celebration " for my own sake ". Mr. Fox of Reading (d. 1738) in his *The Duty of Public Worship Proved* (9th ed. 1771) asks : " Does our Church intend, that the Sacrament should be administered as often as the Communion Service is read ? " and answers Yes. The service is appointed for every Sunday and Holy-day " to remind us of the ancient Church, which received the Sacrament at every opportunity ". On the other hand we find Bishop Burnet (d. 1715) referring to " the too common practice of dead and formal receiving, at the great festivals, as a piece of decency recommended by custom ". Probably, as one manual suggests, the first Sunday in the month was Sacrament Sunday in a large number of town parishes.

The chief hindrances to Communion, other than a sinful life,

---

[1] Sir James Alan Park. Besides " The Holy Communion ", the most usual title, " The Lord's Supper " and " The Holy Sacrament " were commonly used. But " The Eucharist " is frequently to be found.

[2] *Church and State*, pp. 250–55.

were (1) an exaggerated sense of the amount of preparation required, thought by some to entail many hours of meditation and retirement (so Archbishop Synge, of Tuam, died 1742, in *An Answer to all the Excuses and Pretences which Men ordinarily make for their not coming to Holy Communion*); (2) a feeling that reception was inconsistent with a natural tendency to mirth (*ibid.*); (3) the idea that frequent Communion would diminish reverence; and (4) inability to read. *An Earnest Exhortation to a frequent Reception* (first published 1804) quotes Dean Andrews of Canterbury as saying "very few of our sex, in comparison with the other, ever are partakers of the Lord's Supper", and attributing this to sexual indulgence.

The manuals contain very full devotions in preparation for Communion. The directions are founded on "Ye that do truly . . ." —a general holy life, self-examination, restitution of wrong done to others, and charity and faith, are the pre-requisites. See, for example, *The Sacrament of the Lord's Supper explained to the meanest Capacity* (23rd ed. 1818). Self-examination on Friday is taught, repeated on Sunday morning (*A Friendly Call to the Holy Communion*, 1746). Bishop Gibson's manual has many admirable questions in preparation for Communion. "Have I not [1] endeavoured to impose upon my neighbour in matters of trade and traffic, by concealing the faults of my own goods? Have I not taken advantage of his ignorance or his necessities to demand an immoderate price for my own goods, or to allow him too small a consideration for his?" "Do I not secretly wish the death of my parents, out of impatience to be delivered from their government, or possessed of their estate?" "Do I love my wife, and show it in a kind, tender, and gentle behaviour towards her?" He makes the point that self-examination, which is necessary, is in practice very rare except as part of the preparation for Communion.

Bishop Fleetwood of Ely (d. 1723), in *The Reasonable Communicant*, discusses fasting Communion, concluding that light refreshment may be held to be of the nature of fasting. "I do not suppose that any one makes a full meal in the morning, that is not going to strong labour, much less upon Sunday morning." So a light breakfast was usual on weekdays, a specially light one on Sundays.

Coming to the service itself, we find little to remark; all is austerely simple. The first part of the service is said every Sunday, a metrical psalm being sung before and after it. It is very wrong,

---

[1] Note the form of the question (*nonne* not *num*).

says Mrs. Trimmer in *The Teacher's Assistant*, for the choir to sing in such a way that the people cannot join in. Bishop Bull orders a decent interval before the second service; Bishop Gibson, that the space between the services be utilized by the parish clerk, who will read metrical psalms aloud. "There are many helps . . . in the abundance of excellent books published on the Sacrament" (*The Sacrament of the Lord's Supper Explained*). Follow your book closely and join in the prayers, but not audibly, is the universal advice. Communicants sometimes took a devotional book with them to the altar and caused delay by using it after reception. The manuals generally give, besides prayers of preparation and thanksgiving, special devotions for festivals and short ejaculatory prayers. The two main devotional thoughts are renewal of the baptismal covenant and identification with the crucified Saviour.[1] There are prayers " at going up to the altar ", " at giving your alms ", in this order—the communicants being supposed to go up into the chancel at the Offertory. *A Friendly Call* has a prayer after Consecration : " O blessed Jesus, in the bread broken I behold thy Body torn with whips, and thorns, and nails ". *The Sacrament of the Lord's Supper Explained* recommends the reading of the Good Friday Gospel, if the numbers are very great.

The chief motive put before the communicant is the fulfilment of duty. " The Holy Communion, which it will be your duty henceforward to attend " is a typical sentence from *Pastoral Advice to Young Persons before Confirmation*.

As regards doctrinal emphasis, I can find no sign of any belief in the Real Presence in the form often taught today ; the entire emphasis is on the reality of the Gift. Bishop Fleetwood, in *The Reasonable Communicant*, writes : " After the Consecration, such a divine power and efficacy doth accompany the Holy Sacrament, as makes the bread and wine become the spiritual and mystical Body of Christ. . . . The Church of England knows no Corporal Presence, nor any change of the bread and wine into the Natural Body and Blood of Christ." *The Sacrament of the Lord's Supper Explained* says that we receive " in a spiritual and sacramental manner . . . not in a corporeal or bodily manner ".

Peter Waldo, in *An Essay on the Holy Sacrament of the Lord's Supper* (10th ed. 1798), writes : " We are united to Christ, our Head,

---

[1] The outlook is akin to that of the Lutheran Church. In 1909 I visited a Danish Cathedral on a Friday in August, when the Communion was being celebrated. Some sixty or seventy were present, mostly elderly, all dressed in black. The atmosphere was intensely reverent.

and become, in some sense, partakers of the divine Nature ". In
the Consecration Prayer we " beg God's blessing on the elements
of bread and wine, that by the operation of the Holy Spirit, he would
be pleased to make them, to all faithful receivers, in a spiritual
sense, the Body and Blood of Christ ". A prayer in *A Friendly
Call* has the same idea of the infusion of life : " O let that heavenly
food which thou has so lately fed me with, transfuse new life and
new vigour into my soul ". With this may be compared a tract
based on Isaac Barrow, which was reissued as late as 1820. " We,
in the spiritual intention, communicate of his Very Person, being
according to the manner insinuated, intimately united to him."

We may conclude our extracts with some teaching from Archbishop
Wake on the Catechism. " What do you think of the Sacrifice, as
they call it, of the Mass ? " " We do not deny, but that, in a larger
sense, this Sacrament may be called a Sacrifice." The bread and
wine is " altered as to its use, and signification ". " Ought not
Christ to be adored in the Sacrament ? " " Christ is every where
to be adored ; and therefore in the receiving of the Holy Communion, as well as in all other religious practices."

(e) *Confession*

The prevailing view of Confession and Absolution is illustrated
by John Kettlewell's *A Companion for the Penitent* and *The Trial and
Judgment of the Soul* (editions of 1768) ; that Kettlewell was a non-
juror was no obstacle to the circulation of his books by the Society.
The Confession and Absolution in the Communion Service are to be
used, unless the minister prefers the form in the Visitation of the
Sick. The questions apply to any penitent, whether sick or whole ;
an asterisk is added to one question which is only applicable to a sick
man. This implies, as an S.P.C.K. ideal in the eighteenth century,
at least an occasional use of Sacramental Confession on the part of
the whole. Absolution should be followed by the Holy Communion
as soon as possible. Archbishop Hort (Tuam), whose charge was
evidently considered to apply to English conditions as well as Irish,
says that the sick send for the minister " in order to receive the
Communion and Absolution as a sort of passport ".

APOLOGETICS

This is given a section of its own in order to show how small a
place it occupied in the plans of the Society. In the Report for the
year 1800 the names of over 2000 members are printed, headed

by His Royal Highness, George Prince of Wales. The total number of publications on the catalogue was 286, of which some were temporarily out of print. (This does not count various editions of the Bible and the Prayer Book, or books in languages other than English, such as Welsh.) Only five deal in any sense with the evidences of Christianity: Leslie's *Short and Easy Method with the Deists*, Bishop Sherlock's *Trial of the Witnesses of the Resurrection of Jesus* (first published 1729), Bishop Horne's *Letter to Adam Smith*,[1] *A Preservative against the Publications dispersed by Modern Socinians*, and an excellent pamphlet by Bishop Porteous, entitled *Summary of the Principal Evidences for the Truth and Divine Origin of the Christian Religion*, " designed for those lately confirmed in the Diocese of London ". This last is sound and scholarly and shows an appreciation of the fact that the authority of the Bible was no longer unchallenged.

Home Life

This subject is in a measure treated below under the head of various classes of society, and in the chapter on Charity Schools. Here we may mention a few points.

The manuals inculcate an austere piety. *The Religious Instruction of Children Recommended*, by the Rev. Sir James Stonhouse (1774, 8th ed. 1815), is attractive in tone. Gratitude to God for the gift of children and solicitude for the salvation of their souls are the dominant notes. Earnest prayers for the children, gentleness and brevity in instruction, and individual treatment of each child, are urged. *A Regular Method of Governing a Family* (7th ed. 1803) lays stress on the parents' example, daily prayer with the children (" This duty was formerly much more generally observed in this kingdom "), and impartial discipline. Home religious training seems to have been excessive at times by our standards, but gentleness is presupposed. There is no sign of the exaggeration of the fears of hell which was associated with some forms of Evangelism, or of the use of the rod. Perhaps the latter was so much taken for granted that it needed not to be mentioned. But I suspect that most happy homes managed to dispense with it except on rare occasions. White Kennet's *The Excellent Daughter* (16th ed. 1821) was a very popular manual for girls.

All the books contain forms of family prayer. Bishop Gibson's *Family Devotion*, drawn up for the parishioners of Lambeth (new

[1] See p. 105.

edition 1841), was one of the most popular.   One subject for thanksgiving at morning prayer sounds very modern : " To thy watchful
providence we wholly owe it that no disturbance hath come nigh us
or our dwelling ".

MORAL CORRUPTION

It would be tedious to quote continual references to the corruption
of the age, beginning with Bishop Burnet (see p. 22), going on to
the Letter of Bishop Gibson in 1740 urging support of the S.P.C.K.,
in which he says " the decay of piety and religion, and the increase
of sin and vice, are so visible in our days ", and ending with the
" great decay of piety in this corrupt and degenerate age " (*An
Earnest Exhortation to Housekeepers*, 23rd ed. 1819).   " The King's
Proclamation for the Encouragement of Piety and Virtue, and for
Preventing and Punishing of Vice, Profaneness, and Immorality ",
issued in 1787, to be read four times a year in churches, was still being
published by the S.P.C.K. in 1818.[1] It prohibits playing " dice,
cards, or any other game whatsoever " on the Lord's day, urges
attendance at public worship " on pain of Our highest displeasure ",
and the suppression of gaming and disorderly houses, and forbids
the sale of wine, chocolate, coffee, ale etc. during the time of divine
service on Sunday.

Our books are very outspoken in regard to licentiousness.   Bishop
Gibson's *First Pastoral Letter* laments the open vindication of public
stews and mentions " a new sort of vice of a very horrible nature,
and almost unknown in these parts of the world ", which has however
been checked by Government action.   *The Christian Monitor*
frankly discusses venereal disease.   *An Exhortation to Chastity*
(new ed. 1818) urges early marriage in spite of financial difficulties—
it is cheaper than promiscuity.   Drunkenness is treated of in many
books.   Stephen Hales in *A Friendly Admonition to the Drinkers of
Gin, Brandy, and other distilled Spirituous Liquors* (6th ed. 1800)
refers to his experiments on animals, which have proved the harm
done by spirits.   The remedies proposed are the gradual increasing
of the water and decreasing of the dram, and prescriptions to lessen
the craving.   Archbishop Wake and Bishop Gibson give admirable
advice about practical matters.   The former emphasizes the duty
of gentleness and courtesy to children, and of gentleness to servants,
who must not be overworked.   He condemns taking usury from

[1] The Royal Arms are printed on the title page of this edition, an honour
generally confined to the King's Printers.

private persons. Bishop Fleetwood has an interesting dictum on the subject of adultery. " I discharge you from confessing this sin to the abused husband, or to your abused wife ; but I should lay it strictly on you to confess your sin to your wicked partner ", and to try to reclaim him or her.

BIOGRAPHY

Mrs. Trimmer [1] is the best exponent of the art of composing ideal biographies of godly poor men and women, in order to teach morality, but there are some others. Of special interest is the true story of *The Life of William Baker*, a sermon preached at his parish church of Boldre, in Hampshire, in 1791 (new ed. 1825), which shows the incredible frugality of an English peasant. He began work as a boy on 1*d.* a day with food (Jenny of the nursery rhyme, who had the same pay, no doubt had her food too). When he was older he took a field of ten acres. Though employed on a farm, he cultivated his holding by working before sunrise and by moonlight. He kept cows, made his own beer, brought up five children, and supported his sister, and parents-in-law, for whom he built a cottage. In later life he received a legacy consisting of £70 in money and a clock. He settled his children in life with the former and kept the latter. When he was eighty his wife died, and he sold everything, realizing £110, which he invested in an annuity bringing in £8 a year. He spent his old age in preparation for death and in reading the Bible. Everything he possessed that had any value was stolen, but he felt serenely confident in his deprivation. He always had good cheese and bread, home-brewed beer, and cabbages from his garden ; he never tasted fresh meat, butter, or tea, and was never ill. He died at the age of eighty-one, having been regular at church to the end and having never missed the Sacrament.

VARIOUS CLASSES

A curious feature of the literature under review is the extent to which it is aimed at specific classes of the nation—sailors, soldiers, farmers, public-house keepers, and the like. This we avoid as far as possible today, addressing readers as Churchmen or citizens. Remembering the standardization which inevitably follows universal education, we shall probably conclude that different classes, far more than is the case today, had their own standards of conduct and

[1] See p. 118.

manners, and to that extent needed different treatment. Does not the boundless variety of characters portrayed by Dickens reflect English life before the age of democratic standardization?

(a) Servants

Among the manuals for servants are *Serious Advice and Warning to Servants, more especially those of the Nobility and Gentry*, by Thomas Broughton (Secretary of the S.P.C.K., 6th ed. 1809, first published 1746); *A Present for Servants, from their Ministers, Masters, or other Friends* (12th ed. 1821); the first part of *Domestic Happiness promoted in a Series of Discourses from a Father to his Daughter*, by the famous Jonas Hanway (1777); and *A Friendly Gift for Servants and Apprentices* (7th ed. 1823).

A Friendly Gift draws a picture of an ideal servant. She rises early, keeps everything so tidy that she could almost find it in the dark,[1] and is deeply attached to her master, mistress and children—to please God. " She is never seen going about the house with holes in her stockings, or slipshod shoes, or a tattered gown, or blowsy hair, or dirty hands. . . . She wears a stuff gown, or a dark coloured cotton one, and a stuff petticoat." " Her handkerchief is always tidily put on; and pinned close over her neck." She " never desires to go to races, or feasts, or fairs, or any merry makings ". She does not buy silly books or songs, or run after fortune-tellers, or buy lottery-tickets; she finds out the character of her employers before accepting a situation; makes good bargains for her master when shopping, and never accepts presents from tradespeople.

She is urged to take great care with candles. A servant causing a fire is liable to a fine of £100, which if not paid at once is commuted for eighteen months' hard labour. She must not read letters or written papers without leave (it is supposed that she can read). Children must not be praised in their hearing for beauty or clever sayings. Nor must servants say to them things like " the black man shall have you ". Many concrete examples are given, one of which describes a maid who out of her savings paid a fee of £10 10s to a surgeon for an operation on her father.

Jonas Hanway warns maids coming to London against falling into the hands of procuresses, especially telling them to beware of public registry offices. *The Young Woman's Monitor* gives similar warnings—profligate men servants are a great danger. Dr. Broughton

---

[1] Not an exaggeration, see p. 132. Before modern methods of illumination many must have cultivated this gift.

says that drunkenness, fornication, and gaming, are the three great sins of men servants, in which they only copy their masters. Indeed we have only to think of the conditions which must have prevailed in a great London house, with a score or more of men and women packed into the attics, probably well if coarsely fed, and with access to plenty of alcoholic liquor, to realize the danger to morals.

A different and very painful picture is drawn in *A Present for Servants*, which purports to deal not with the servants of rich men, or with slaves, but with those who have hired themselves out because of poverty. Even these have a good deal of leisure, and much of Sunday to themselves. Servants oppressed by rigour and unjust severity must be submissive. "To be laid in some cold out-house, or meanest loft of a poor cottage ; to have the leavings of the coarse fare there ; hard work, cold blasts abroad, and perhaps hard words and unkind usage at home ; this grates upon the spirit, and makes them think their life more miserable than any other." But contrast your lot with that of the Christian slaves at Algiers ! True, but one wishes the writer had not added : " How free is the servant's life, and void of those troubles to which even your own masters and others that live around you are frequently exposed. They have great rents to pay, and the money hardly got to pay them with ; they have meat and drink to provide for you, and wages at the year's end ; one trespasses upon their fields, and another deprives them of their debts."

(b) Soldiers

The Christian Soldier, an address given in 1737 to a military audience in the Tower of London, reached its 42nd edition in 1818. It is obvious that soldiers had a bad reputation in respect of morals, which was only too much justified by the facts. Broken men enlisted as a last resort. (Compare *An Earnest and Affectionate Address to the Poor against Drunkenness*, new ed. 1818. By frequenting the alehouse you will come to poverty ; " you will enlist as a common soldier, and throw your children on the parish".) The preacher enlarged on the example of the New Testament soldier Cornelius. Drunkenness and uncleanness are their chief sins. " You assemble by troops in tippling houses ", keeping up your revels and obscene songs till midnight. " My brethren, Cornelius did not so." " Your offences, in point of chastity, are very scandalous, and too notorious to be denied ; insomuch that the bare sight of you is suspicious and painful to the modest part of the daughters of our land." Soldiers pawn accoutrements for their lust, and venereal disease is rife among them.

The Soldier's Monitor, by Josiah Woodward, which was given away to Marlborough's soldiers, reached its 30th edition in 1802.

(c) Sailors

Sailors ranked with soldiers. Penalties were enforced by law against swearing, on the following scale : " Labourers, soldiers and sailors, one shilling ; others below gentlemen, two shillings ; gentlemen and above, five shillings ". A popular pamphlet designed for sailors was *The Sailor's Monitor, or Advice to Seafaring Men*, by Josiah Woodward, " published by His Majesty's Special Command " (21st ed. 1818); it lays great stress on ejaculatory prayer, often the only form possible on board ship. *An Old Chaplain's Farewell Letter* (new ed. 1815) says that the writer served from 1793 to 1801 on a ship of the Royal Navy, and then retired to a country living in Staffordshire. The style is charming ; so is the picture he draws of his recognizing seafaring men as they roll along the road and of his entertaining them. The grim side of this rough century appears in *A Kind Admonition to all Seafaring Persons against Mutiny and Piracy*. If you become pirates, you will never see your native country again, never stay long in one place.

(d) Public-House Keepers

The Public Housekeeper's Monitor (new ed. 1793) reveals a state of license. Laws are strict enough, but in the absence of any but a rudimentary police are not enforced. They forbid unlawful games—cards, dice, draughts, shuffle-board, Mississippi or billiard tables, skittles, and nine pins ; as well as raffles. Also selling ale in unmarked measures or allowing tippling. A tippler (the word is not defined) is put in the stocks for four hours, a drunkard for six.

The great temptation of the publican was to keep a house of ill fame, so we are told, perhaps in order to make a living, for few towns were not overstocked with public-houses. Other faults castigated are drinking with guests, putting them into damp beds, not feeding their beasts, opening for midnight revels, and letting customers run up scores. There is no suggestion that total abstinence is desirable, and spirits rather than beer are looked upon as the enemy. No. I of *Tracts upon Practical Subjects* (about 1830) has an edifying story. " A well-known brewer attributed his success to the liberality with which he used his malt . . . the brewer put his character into the beer, and it proved generous accordingly . . . which laid the foundation of a large fortune."

(e) Farmers etc.

A popular devotional book was *The Husbandman's Manual, directing him how to improve the several Actions of his Calling, and the most usual Occurrences of his Life, to the Glory of God and the Benefit of his Soul* (1694, 18th ed. 1799. Anon., by Edward Welchman). It breathes a spirit of simple piety which must have ennobled many humble lives. Prayers and meditations are provided for such occasions as ploughing and sowing, planting and grafting, hearing the cock crow, beekeeping, or watching the movements of ants. The mower is told to imagine himself Death cutting down human lives. Rent day should remind you of your final account with God.

The Husbandman's Spiritual Companion takes a similar line. There are also *The Country Clergyman's Advice to his Parishioners* (anon., by William Holmes) and *The Country Gentleman's Advice to his Neighbours* (12th ed. 1795). The latter tackles the sins of the more fortunate classes—adultery, the keeping of a mistress, etc. He attacks the vice of gaming,[1] unknown in the villages, though it has of late crept into the country towns (he must mean gaming as practised on the scale of the aristocracy), and reveals the continuance of primitive ideas (or was it the surviving influence of the civil marriages of the Commonwealth period?). Some think "that if they keep to one woman only, living with her in all respects as a husband with a wife, the matrimonial ceremony may be safely omitted, as a mere human institution ".

(f) Prisoners

A Plain and Serious Exhortation to Prisoners, both Debtors and Criminals (new ed. 1813) refers to the amazing increase in the prison population, and urges the segregation of prisoners into debtors, criminals confined for small offences, and those condemned to death. Debtors are in prison because of imprudence or debauchery. Small crimes are committed mostly by raw and inexperienced youths. Much space is given to those who must prepare for death, under the guidance of the chaplain. The S.P.C.K. form for this and other

[1] The naïvety of religious people, by our standards, is illustrated by the remark of *A Disswasive from Gaming* (anon., Josiah Woodward) : " We find nothing like these vanities in the lives of the holy patriarchs."

purposes connected with prisoners was the *Form of Prayer for the Visitation of Prisoners treated upon by the Archbishops and Bishops and the rest of the Clergy* [1] *of the Church of Ireland, and agreed upon by Her Majesty's License in their Synod, holden at Dublin, in the year 1711.* Apparently the Irish Church had more initiative in these matters.

(g) Smugglers

The Duty of Paying Custom (new ed. 1818) deals with the equivalent of our modern "black market"; the "duty" is enjoined by revelation. Dealers in goods on which the tax has not been paid undersell the honest trader, who is driven out of business or forced to follow suit for his family's sake. Those who buy are equally guilty, as receivers. You say you ask no questions : the price, the character of the seller, the secrecy, all warn you. The high duties levied on imported goods, the opportunities of landing on the south coast on dark nights, the absence of modern methods of communication and of a proper police, must have made smuggling easy. Without it our historical romances would be poorer, but the reality was sordid enough.

Two matters not easily classified may be mentioned here. Curious sidelights are thrown on the survival of popular superstitions and customs. *A serious Address to Godfathers and Godmothers* (new ed. 1799) explains renouncing the Devil as "renouncing all dealings with the Devil, whether by practising witchcraft ourselves, or by going to witches and conjurers for assistance, or consulting them upon any occasion whatever". *An Earnest and Affectionate Address to the Common People of England concerning their usual Recreations on Shrove Tuesday* (new ed. 1800. Anon., by Dean Tucker of Gloucester) condemns the abominable practice of throwing at cocks, and expresses a wish that pitching the bar, throwing the sledge or a weighty stone, and leaping and wrestling, were more in use.

THE CLERGY

Five works were adopted by the S.P.C.K. as the standard books for those in or contemplating Holy Orders. *A Discourse of the Pastoral Care*, by Bishop Gilbert Burnet, can be read with profit still. The Preface to the third edition, dated November 15th, 1712, is pessimistic indeed. " I cannot look on, without the deepest concern, when I see imminent ruin hanging over this Church . . . the outward state of things is bad enough, God knows "; but the

[1] Note the accuracy of the phrasing.

inward is worse. "Our Ember weeks are the burden and grief of my life." Candidates are ignorant of the Bible and can't even say the Catechism. Those who come to be instituted have lost what little knowledge they had. Politics and party strife have eaten the heart out of religion. "Scandal" is rare, but an "unthinking course of life, with little or no application to study . . . is but too common". The original Preface said that Popish priests had recovered respect and the Reformation of Popery had stopped the other Reformation. Pastoral care, he goes on to say, has been neglected in the Church of England. One cause of the growing atheism and impiety here and in Europe is the low opinion of the clergy, in whom men do not see strictness of life, contempt of the world, or zeal. The clergyman's diversions ought to be his friends and his garden. The Collects, Psalms, and New Testament, should be learned by heart. Preach catechetical sermons, lasting fifteen minutes, in the afternoon. Visit the sick diligently, not waiting till you are sent for. The Bishop is content to recommend an hour a day of ordinary visiting two or three times a week.[1] Clerical meetings should be held four or five times during the summer. The whole Discourse is a revelation to those who think of the Bishop as a typical Latitudinarian and political prelate.

Little is known by the ordinary student about preparation for Holy Orders during the century. Valuable information is found in *Directions for Young Students in Divinity, with regard to those Attainments, which are necessary to qualify them for Holy Orders* (2nd ed. 1773), by Henry Owen, Chaplain to Shute Barrington, Bishop of Llandaff. This book is directed to those who have no University education, but are left to themselves. The ordinand must renounce worldly concerns, meditate frequently, and have definite seasons of fasting and prayer. The books recommended are those which can for the most part be borrowed. Let the student begin with Tully's *Offices*, Plutarch, Seneca, Epictetus, and Marcus Aurelius. Juvenal and other poets are useful, but must be read with care. Xenophon's *Life of Socrates* is the best book of pagan antiquity. Of Christian moralists, More's *Ethics*, Taylor's *Holy Living and Holy Dying*, and Law's *Serious Call*, are specially recommended. The Bible is the main subject of study, and a copy with good references should be used. The New Testament must be read in the original; Grotius, Le Clerc, Patrick, and Lowth, are the most important writers on the Bible. For dogmatics Pearson on the Creed, Secker's

---

[1] Probably sufficient in a small parish, where the clergyman was resident and continually mixing with the people.

Catechetical Lectures, Burnet's *Exposition*, and of course Hooker, must be studied. Ordinands must form the habit of reading two sermons every Sunday, especially from the works of Tillotson, Sharp, Atterbury, Sherlock, and Secker, the last being the most useful. " The Archbishop of Cambray's *Dialogue on Eloquence* " must not be neglected, and Wheatly on the Common Prayer is the best liturgical authority.

Bishop Bull, of St. David's, in his *Companion for the Candidates of Holy Orders*, recommends the study of " casuistical divines ".

William Paley's Ordination Sermon of July 29th, 1781, published by the S.P.C.K. as *Advice Addressed to the Young Clergy*, went into a new edition in 1813. Paley bids them compare their lot with that of incumbents : you have no disputes about rights or legal dues and are on a level with the greatest part of your parishioners. The virtues inculcated are : (1) *frugality*—the young clergyman must practise " economy on a plan " ; he has enough for his wants and decencies, no more ; (2) *sobriety* ; (3) *avoidance* of dissoluteness—an unchaste connexion on the part of a clergyman will debauch a whole neighbourhood ; (4) *retirement*—learn to live alone and resist impatience of solitude ; avoid public houses, where you will be affronted by coarse jests ; (5) *seriousness of demeanour*, especially in taking services.

The primary visitation charge of Archbishop Hort of Tuam, 1742, was circulated in England. It urges frugality ; the clergyman should set aside one-fourth of his income to provide for his old age, and for his widow and dependents.

The number and quality of the books which come under the head of *Pastor in Parochia* provide a corrective of preconceived ideas. *A New Manual of Devotion* (29th ed. 1824) is the most elaborate, running to about 300 pages. It provides private prayers varying with each day of the week, morning, noon and night ; prayers for children, servants etc. ; ejaculations ; offices of humiliation to be used with the sick or prisoners, and of preparation for Holy Communion ; and forms of self-examination far fuller than would be thought desirable today. The long lists of questions given in nineteenth century books, from which we have reacted, merely continue the Anglican tradition. One intercession is for all religious Societies, including those for Propagating the Gospel in Foreign Parts and for Promoting Christian Knowledge at Home.[1]

---

[1] This formula is used in an S.P.C.K. edition, dated 1821, of a book by Bishop Wilson, see p. 142.

Many manuals provide for the needs of sick visiting. *A Discourse concerning a Deathbed Repentance*, by W. Assheton (16th ed. 1825), gives very careful instructions as to dealing with the dying, with lines of reply to the various objections raised to the minister's exhortations. The state of mind of the average Englishman when death approaches seems not to have changed at all since the eighteenth century. A very elaborate work on the same lines is *Death Bed Scenes and Pastoral Conversations* in three volumes (4th ed. 1830. Anon., by John Warton).

CONTROVERSY

This is very scantily represented. Such as there is, is directed against Papists and Methodists. Bishop Porteous' *Letter to the Clergy of the Diocese of Chester* (1781) contains some interesting figures. In 1767 there were 67,716 Papists; in 1780, 69,376, of which number 27,228 were found in his diocese. The few conversions are due to (1) bribes, (2) inter-marriage, (3) the influence of Roman Catholic masters and mistresses, (4) the cheaper fees charged by R.C. schools.

A widely circulated pamphlet was *A sincere Christian and Convert from the Church of Rome, as exemplified in the Life of Daniel Hersey, a poor Irish Peasant*, by Archbishop Synge, of Tuam (new ed. 1757). The hero saved a halfpenny a day, until he was able to purchase two cows and nine sheep. He took land and paid rent at first, afterwards doing twenty days' work for the landlord during the year in lieu of rent. The poor fellow had been brought up on such books as *The Seven Wise Masters*, *The History of Fortunatus*, *Gesta Romanorum*, *Valentine and Orson*, *The Seven Champions of Christendom*, etc.—surely a more liberal education than that enjoyed by a poor English peasant! He found a Bible, confuted the priest with its aid, married a Protestant, and joined the Church of Ireland.

Only two entries in the 1800 list of S.P.C.K. books are concerned with Methodism and Enthusiasm: *An Earnest and Affectionate Address to Methodists* [1] and Bishop Gibson's *Caution against Enthusiasm*. The word is of course used in the current sense, of claiming special gifts of the Holy Ghost.[2] The Methodists are said to have seized pulpits without leave, preached in unlicensed places such as fields

---

[1] Anon., by Henry Stebbing.

[2] Gibson defines it as " a strong persuasion . . . that they are guided in an extraordinary manner, by immediate impulses and impressions of the Spirit of God ". His book *The Evil and Danger of Lukewarmness in Religion* (19th ed. 1819) shows his pastoral zeal.

C

and commons, and administered the consecrated elements with the words " The Body (Blood) of our Lord Jesus Christ " only. One negative piece of evidence is worth recording. Not till I reached *Death Bed Scenes* (1830) did I find any reference to Evangelicalism. An Evangelical lady visitor is said to have upset the women in the almshouse by saying that the Vicar preached only morality. The Church of England, in so far as it was represented by the S.P.C.K., got on without internal controversy, except where the extreme Latitudinarian wing, shading off into Unitarianism, was concerned.

FOREIGN MISSIONS

Another remarkable silence is to be noted in regard to missions. The East Indian Mission, with its Lutheran missionaries, was apparently considered a kind of annex to the main work of the Society. In Henry Newman's time it was supported by a special fund, which had its own treasurer. Such missionary interest as appears in our books is concerned with America—I have found no reference to India. A manual of instruction for the American Indians was on the list for many years.

The earnestness and the limitations of the eighteenth century are well illustrated by two little books on slavery. The first is *Two Sermons preached to a Congregation of Black Slaves at the Parish Church of S. P. in the Province of Maryland*, by an American Pastor (1749). S. P. is St. Peter, Talbot County, and the preacher is Thomas Bacon. In the Preface, which is addressed to the Whites, he says : " At the conclusion of each sermon, when you were retired into the churchyard, your general remark was,—' If these poor creatures would but mind, and do as the minister told them today, they would make excellent slaves.' "

A special obligation rests upon him to preach to the slaves, for the clergy in Maryland are supported by a poll tax, by which slaves above sixteen pay as much as their masters. He has preached to them at funerals, marriages, and at his own house on both Sunday and weekday evenings. But owing to distance many are unreached. The exhortations to the negroes are earnest and simple.

> My dear black brethren and sisters. . . . Think within yourselves what a terrible thing it would be, after all your labours and sufferings in this life, to be turned into hell in the next life :—and after wearing out your bodies in service here, to go into a far worse slavery when this is over, and your souls be delivered over into the possession of the devil, to become his slaves for ever in hell. . . . Your bodies are not your own. . . . But your precious souls are still your own.

Most of his hearers are baptized. They must remember that faults committed against masters are faults against God himself, who has made them his overseers. Faithful service is required by the law of Christ.

> Suppose you were masters and mistresses and had servants under you . . . would you not desire that your servants should do their business faithfully and honestly, as well when your back was turned, as while you were looking over them ? . . . You well know, that there are many among you so fond of rambling, that unless there be some revelling at home, they are seldom or never to be found at night in their own masters' houses or quarters :—but as soon as it is dark, take the first horse they can get, either master's or neighbour's, and after spending the whole night in revelling and drunkenness, and riding the poor creatures about to death, come home by day, dull, heavy and drowsy, unfit to do any business as it ought to be done. . . .
>
> If the week days afford you very little leisure, the Sundays at least are your own in a great measure . . . confirmed to you by the laws of the country.

As regards punishment, the good minister uses an argument familiar to the older generation of readers from schoolboy experience : Either you deserve it, or you do not—if the latter, then it was a recompense for occasions when you deserved punishment and were not detected.

So much for the slaves. Four sermons preached to the masters were published in 1750 by the same priest. The negroes under the skin are the same as the whites, not, as some argue, an intermediate species between man and beast. They are to be brought to the font, and the whites must be sponsors, for there are no black communicants. The common fear of baptism is groundless. " We have an express Act of Assembly in this Province declaring, that *slaves, when baptized, do remain slaves still*, so that whatever rights or privileges they acquire by being made Christians, do all belong to another life." The Roman Catholics think it an honour to stand for their slaves. The baptized slaves must be carefully trained and taught. Evening classes at the master's house are recommended. When slaves live at a distance, catechists should be employed. If the ordinary schoolmasters are unwilling to do the work, " I will undertake . . . to have one or more catechists properly qualified to be sent over and recommended by the Society for Promoting Christian Knowledge, of which I have the honour, though unworthy, to be a corresponding member ".

The publication of these sermons in England by the S.P.C.K. shows the interest taken in American problems. Mr. Bacon did his best, but the state of things here revealed is sufficient explanation of the fact that, when an opportunity for choice was given, the negroes almost universally chose a form of Christianity other than the Church of their masters.

CONCLUSIONS

If we try to sum up the lessons of our survey, these results appear.

1. The Church of England is generally described as having been complacent in the eighteenth century. Of this there is not the slightest sign in our sources. We get an impression of a militant Church, fighting for its life against unbelief and coarse and dissolute manners, depressed at times by the magnitude of its task, but fully conscious both of the evil it was facing and of its impotence to face it in its own strength. The impression is as strong at the beginning as at the end.

2. The main weapon used is the quoting of Scripture texts. They are common ground to the Churchman, the Dissenter, the Socinian or Deist (whose claim was that his interpretation of the New Testament was the true one), even the unchurched masses. Only towards the end of the century was there any perception that the whole fabric of Christianity was threatened. In spite of the close ties between France and England, when not interrupted by war, the writers of Anglican books do not seem to have taken Voltaire seriously.

3. There is no sign of any desire to improve the Prayer Book. It stands by the side of the Bible as a document to be accepted without question and to be commented on minutely. I have not found the phrase " our incomparable liturgy ".

4. In regard to dogma, singularly little is said about the Incarnation, the Resurrection, or the Holy Spirit. Evangelical phraseology about the Atonement was little used. All is orderly ; " the plan of salvation " is so completely presupposed that there is no need to dilate on what nobody doubts.

5. The last conclusion may excite surprise. These eighteenth century writers with hardly an exception have an admirable English style. When we begin to read them we may find it wooden and featureless, so accustomed are we to writing for effect. As we read on we realize how good the English is. The writers are uniformly lucid and vigorous ; they know when to make a break in an argument by means of an illustration or a story. One reason for

their success is that their objective was limited, there was no need for
the aim to exceed the grasp. But they never write down to the
assumed level of their illiterate readers. Continually we feel that
the contents and manner would be over the heads of the educated
democracy of today. We cannot suppose that all this literature,
distributed for a hundred years by intelligent people, was useless
for its purpose. Rather we must conclude that there was no great
gulf between the English of the writers and the natural dignity of
the untutored speech of the masses, still to a large extent based, as
in Bunyan's time, on the Bible and the Prayer Book.

This survey has confined itself to pastoral-hearted Anglicans, who
believed in the Church of England and tried their best to make the
Prayer Book work. One feels the decline from the fervours of the
seventeenth century. But even the most convinced of Anglicans
must find other things lacking. On the one hand the common
people of England had lost the bright colourful life of mediaeval
religion, closely linked with the processes of nature. A largely
successful attempt had been made to banish superstition, but how
much that was good and beautiful went with it ! On the other hand
in the Prayer Book religion I have described the emotions were, if
not starved, at least not adequately fed. It is sufficient to mention
Charles Wesley's hymns to show what is absent from our documents.

II

HENRY NEWMAN 1670–1743

I HAVE lived so long with the subject of this sketch, whose private as well as business letters are preserved in the archives of the S.P.C.K., that the opportunity of introducing him to my readers gives me peculiar pleasure. For many years I have at intervals read his correspondence and now I can share my knowledge with others. He deserves a full-length biography, but that would demand research for which I have neither time nor inclination. Newman touched life at many points. A New England business man, he came to live in London, and was appointed Secretary of the S.P.C.K., but never relinquished his ties of friendship and business with his old home. He acted as agent for one of the Colonies, corresponded with many of the Governors, played a large part in the arrangements for sending persecuted Protestants to Georgia, was concerned with the relief of Huguenots, managed the London affairs of many country friends, befriended humble people and wrote letters on their behalf to high officials—all this besides being an indefatigable Secretary of a Society whose work was mainly concerned with Charity Schools and the distribution of Christian literature.

The full story must be left to one who will investigate the Newman papers among the Rawlinson MSS. in the Bodleian Library at Oxford, the Colonial Office Papers, and similar documents; and will use whatever evidence is to be found in America.[1] My purpose is to give a picture of the man as he lives again in his correspondence, designedly incomplete so as to induce someone else to tell the whole story. Perhaps it has come easier to a successor of Newman in the Secretary's office to understand him than it would have done to an outsider.

Thanks to the generous help of the Pilgrim Trust the archives of the Society are now properly arranged, having been put into order by Miss F. M. Burkett. The Newman letters are in the form of the drafts written in his own hand, to be copied by the clerk. They are in fifty-two volumes, indexed at the time. My task has been made easier by the typed copies of the more important letters made

---

[1] The *Dictionary of American Biography*, which has an article on Newman, refers to a sketch in J. L. Sibley's *Biographical Sketches of Graduates of Harvard University* (1885), iii. 389–94. I have not had access to this.

by Miss Burkett, a few of whose notes I have used. I have followed the punctuation and spelling of the original, with negligible exceptions, but not the erratic capitalization. Abbreviations have been written out in full.

I. An Outline of Newman's Life

Newman's grandfather, Samuel Newman, appears in the *Dictionary of National Biography*,[1] which draws its information from Cotton Mather's *Magnalia Christi Americana*, the *Athenae Oxonienses*, and histories of New England. These sources can be supplemented from Henry Newman's recollections.

He was born at or near Chadlington, a village in Oxfordshire, about 1600, of an eminent Protestant family, and went to Magdalen College, Oxford, as a servitor in 1617; he migrated to St. Edmund Hall, from which he took his B.A. in 1620. Cotton Mather describes him as an eminent Biblical scholar,[2] who compiled the most elaborate concordance yet made in Europe, enlarging it still further after settling in America. " Thou, Newman, hast excelled them all." He was presumably ordained, and took a strongly Puritan line. " The Episcopal molestations compelled him to no less than seven removes." He sailed in 1638 and spent the rest of his life in settlements around Boston : $1\frac{1}{2}$ years in Dorchester, 5 in Weymouth, and 19 in Rehoboth, to which place he gave its name. He was a very lively preacher, a hard student, and given to hospitality. He died in 1663 with these words on his lips : " And now, ye Angels of the Lord Jesus Christ, come, do your office ". The loss of his diary accounts for Mather's having less to say about him than about many of his contemporaries.

Henry Newman wrote an unfinished letter to the Rev. Thomas Prince of Boston, dated July 16th, 1729,[3] giving an account of his life up to 1698. The part concerning his grandfather was intended only to supplement the account in the *Magnalia*.

My grandfather was born at Banbury in Oxfordshire and educated at Oxford as the author of the Magnalia observes, and afterwards he went into Yorkshire and preach'd in the vicarage of Halifax as I have been inform'd here till the persecutions of the Puritans under the Laudean faction oblig'd him to retire to New England but in what year any of these occurrences happen'd I'm not able to say.

[1] But not in the American Dictionary.
[2] *Magnalia Christi Americana* (1702), III. 113 ff. The chapter is headed " Bibliander Nov. Anglicanus ".
[3] No adjustment has been made in any of these letter dates for "old style ".

Unfortunately, when Newman came to England his father's memoirs were lost in a coasting ship which took his baggage from Portsmouth to London, so he had to trust to memory. Banbury probably means that the family moved to that town from Chadlington. Halifax means the chapelry of Cross Stone in the large parish of that name, some twelve miles west of the town, where Samuel Newman was preacher in 1622–23. This, probably his first cure, was the only one to be remembered.[1]

He had three sons Antipas Samuel and Noah. *Antipas* was I believe born at Weymouth and liv'd to be minister of Wenham and had two sons John and Samuel the last of whom died in the West Indies, the eldest was sometime Representative for the town of Wenham. *Samuel* liv'd and dy'd a plain usefull layman at Rehoboth leaving two sons Samuel and David. *Noah* was born at Rehoboth, about the year 1646, where he was educated under his father and liv'd to succeed him, though not immediately because he could not be above 17 year old when his father dy'd supposing that he dy'd as Dr. Mather's History mentions in 1663. Noah after his being settl'd as his father's successor marry'd Mrs. Joanna Flint, a daughter of the Revd. Mr. Henry Flint of Roxbury about the year 1669, by whom he had 3 children, viz: Henry, born the 10th of November 1670,[2] and Samuel and Mary who dy'd young. Noah dy'd of a consumption about 1678 leaving only his wife who dy'd of a consumption about a year afterward, and Henry to the care of a benign Providence.

Henry, then, was the son of a Congregationalist minister and had no brothers or sisters, but, as we shall see, a number of cousins.

Henry was put to school at Roxbury, Dorchester, Dedham and last of all at Braintree under the guardianship of Mrs. Flint his grandmother, Mr. Benjamin Tompson being his master at this last place when he was sent to Harvard College 1683 before he was qualify'd for it (during Mr. Rogers's Presidentship) Mrs. Flint being very desirous to see him and other of her grandchildren push'd into the world before she left it.[3] He was design'd by his friends for the ministry but his want of several qualifications and his genius [4] strongly inclining him to travel instead of studying theology he learn'd the French language, read cheifly mathematical books [5] and travels after he had taken his first degree at Cambridge and acquir'd the French language by spending a summer at the French town of Narragansett that he might be ready to ramble when opportunity offer'd.

[1] Halifax Antiquarian Society Proceedings 1928. Reference kindly provided by the Chief Librarian of Halifax.
[2] *The Dictionary of American Biography* gives Nov. 20th, making allowance for old style.
[3] Bachelor of Arts 1687, Master 1690 (*Dict. of Am. Biogr.*).
[4] He omits to refer to his attraction to the Church of England.
[5] Especially astronomy. He published *Harvard's Ephemeris* in 1690, and *News from the Stars* in 1691 (*Dict. of Am. Biogr.*).

Newman gives two pieces of information about his boyhood. " When I went to school I learnt from some of my playfellows to say *Odzuckers, Oddsliffikins, the Dickens is in it,* and *the Duce take it,* not knowing the tendency of these phrases to oaths and curses, but those who had the care of my education, I thank 'em, soon convinced me of my error, and taught me to keep at the utmost distance from expressions so unbecoming a Christian and a gentleman " (Jan. 7th, 1724). And he contrasts the dusty books of St. Martin's library, founded by Archbishop Tenison, with the order of Harvard. " When I liv'd at Harvard College and was honour'd with the care of the public library . . . I was ambitious of nothing more than to keep it clean, that strangers particularly Sir Francis Wheeler and the officers of his squadron when they saw it confess'd they never saw a College library at Oxford or Cambridge in England come up to it, and when I afterwards came to England I was surpriz'd to find many College libraries inferior to ours, in all respects " (Nov. 20th, 1740, Rev. Mr. Colman, Boston). The standard of education at Harvard was high from the first.

There are many references to American cousins : Henry Flint of Harvard, Edmund and Josiah Quincy [1] (merchants of Boston), the wife of Nathaniel Sparhawk of Cambridge, the wife of the Rev. Mr. Wetmore of Eye, and John Winthrop. These are evidently on his mother's side, or else descendants of Samuel Newman through his daughters. A son of his cousin John Newman came over to England in 1737. One of the last letters Henry Newman wrote refers to 145 acres of land at Rehoboth which belong to him ; also to his relations there. To continue the autobiography.

In 1692 he was invited by Mr. Marston of Salem the owner of a ship commanded by John Beal of Marblehead to take a voyage to Bilbao in Spain in a merchant ship of which he was cheif owner, this invitation was very acceptable his duty being only to read prayers and on Sundays a sermon to the crew. At this time it was he apply'd himself to understand the art of navigation and whatever else might qualify him for business. He went 3 voyages to Bilbao in this ship and tho' in every voyage the ship was engag'd with French ships and lost men she always clear'd her self of 'em by the bravery of the Captain and his men and afterward made an agreeable tour back to New England as once by the way of Cadiz, another time by the Cape de Verde Islands Barbadoes and Tortugas and the last voyage 1694 he got leave at Bilbao the latter end of 1694 to embark in the Falkland commanded by Captain Long to England where upon his arrival at Falmouth some distance from the

[1] The original Edmund and Judith Quincy sailed to Massachusetts with the Rev. John Cotton in 1633.

town he prostrated himself upon the ground to kiss it and with humble thanks to God for having preserv'd him through so many storms and engagements with French ships. In one of which he was wounded in the thigh by a smal shot and at last to bring him to the land of his forefathers which he had so long impatiently wish'd to see. Some of the boat's crew that were with him thinking he had been in a fit run up to him to know what was the matter, which he soon explain'd to 'em by kissing every post and tree as they past on to the town.

Being arriv'd in London, he found with few letters of recommendation many friends and in a few months soon after he was invited to a partnership with Mr. Francis Taylor who had liv'd some years as a merchant at Stockholm, to go with him to Newfoundland, in behalf of a Company at London to negotiate as factors a stock of ten thousand pounds propos'd to be circulated from London to New England and thence in provisions to Newfoundland the produce of which to be remitted either directly to England or in fish etc. to Spain and Portugal, but his project was soon laid aside by the news of the French having destroy'd the principal settlements of the English, and therefore after about 15 months stay in London he return'd with a cargo of about 500 £ sterling on commission to Boston where he comenced merchant 1696, and by that time he had spent a year there the same project of settling a factory at Newfoundland was reviv'd at London upon the Peace at Reswick, and Mr. Taylor following him to Boston Articles of Partnership for 7 year were there agreed on and both proceeded in different sloops laden with provisions to St. Johns Newfoundland 1698.

The letter ends abruptly and we are left with a gap of a few years. Newman is mentioned in the Colonial Office Papers of 1701 as " Register " at St. John's, Newfoundland, and in one of his later letters he speaks of Newfoundland, " which claims the preference in respect of wildness of all places ". On May 13th, 1703, he first appears in the S.P.C.K. Minutes, being appointed correspondent for Newfoundland. He attended his first meeting on June 3rd and during the next four years was frequently present, so that he must have been in England during that time. Mr. Humphrey Wanley,[1] the Anglo-Saxon scholar, was Secretary of the Society from 1702 to 1708, when he retired to become Secretary of the Society of Antiquaries. Newman took his place on June 24th, 1708. A characteristic letter is preserved in which he replies to the invitation.[2]

There is nothing could have been more agreable to my inclinations, thus to serve the Committee of the Society in what you propos'd were I free from another engagement which happens at present to engross so much of my time that I must not pretend in any tollerable manner

[1] For Wanley see the chapter devoted to him in D. C. Douglas, *English Scholars*.

The Revd. Mr. Shute, March 25th, 1708.

to be capable of executing both. And I must own if I had been free tho' the business it self had been most agreable yet I should have found some difficulty to accept a salary from the Society out of what is collected for pious uses.

He proceeds to suggest that the work of the Society should be shared between four or six gentlemen, each serving for two or three months ; the paid staff to consist of a messenger and a Charity School boy.

> Some such expedient as this would in 7 years time save near 500 £, which, with their usual management, would erect a great many schools, or purchase not a few books. And if, as I am promis'd, the summer affords me much leisure, I shall be proud to devote it all to the service of the Society, that if possible I might atone for the unprofitableness of,
> Sir,
> Your most obedient humble servant.

The most probable inference is that a salary of £70 a year was proposed ; Mr. Wanley is stated in one place to have received £40. The actual salary paid to Newman was £60.

From 1708 to his death on June 15th, 1743, Newman's story is that of the Society and of the other works in which he was engaged. He lived in rooms in Whitehall [1] until 1714 when " a gentleman of the Temple having made a present of his chambers to my masters they have given me the use of them whilst I am in their service and therefore I intend to move thither ". His letters are headed Middle Temple until 1728, when the Society acquired an office in Bartlet's Buildings. In 1716 he refused an invitation to become Secretary of another body as well as of the S.P.C.K. " Whoever undertakes it ought to speak and write Latin like an angel, but I can do neither. He ought to understand French Italian Spanish and High Dutch if not to speak them, but how little do I know of these languages." I have no suggestion to make as to the identity of this body, unless Newman changed his mind and the reference is to the Commissioners for relieving Poor Proselytes, on whose behalf he submitted a Report to the Bishop of London in 1719.[2] He wrote to Lord Perceval [3] thanking him for his offer to lend £100 " towards entituling them to a subscription in the South Sea for the benefit of the Proselytes. . . . It would not be for the

[1] " My chamber up the Chappel Stairs in Whitehall " (June 4th, 1713).
[2] The work, which was associated with, but not formally undertaken by, the S.P.C.K., would require a knowledge of languages. The Society has some of the documents.
[3] Sept. 8th, 1720.

honour of the Society to engage in such a way of raising money for them." It was a thankless task, and he submitted a memorandum to the Commissioners in October 1723, suggesting that they should resign in a body. Those relieved are generally a disgrace to any communion. The Royal Bounty of £15,000 a year attracts the dregs of the Church of Rome, and as many as fifty French spies have been detected. His advice was taken.

In the same year Newman just missed a great honour. The Archbishop of Canterbury and the Bishop of London used their influence to have him made Secretary of Queen Anne's Bounty. But the Treasurer of Q.A.B. asked for the post on grounds of health and got it. The Governors then unanimously recommended Newman for the post of Treasurer; it was an office held by patent from the Crown, and the holder had to find security for £30,000– £40,000. The recommendation was not accepted. In 1721 we find Newman organizing the relief of captives lately returned from Barbary and writing on their behalf to the Secretary of the Admiralty—to supplement " the common necessities allowed to them by the Government ".

There are occasional references to his domestic habits. He writes to a friend [1] saying that nearly every day he dines or sups with his son and they discuss religion or philosophy. " I go once a week to St. Dunstan's Coffee House—on Tuesday mornings." [2] He drank milk for breakfast, evidently an unusual practice, to judge by the number of times he recommends it. Mixed with boiling water and sugar " with a slice of brown bread and butter [it] is a good breakfast for any man that does not labour much, and intends to have a good appetite for dinner ". After nearly dying of pleurisy in 1722, he restored his health by riding on Hampstead Heath; in 1734 he refers to " excursions abroad now and then on horseback to get rid of the scurvey sedentary life has subjected me to ". Finally he had recourse to the automatic chamber horse, patronized by " Princess Amelia and several people of quality ", which cost him £3 11s. 6d. In the last period of his life he was a martyr to asthma.

II. THE SECRETARY OF S.P.C.K.

A Committee of Inquiry into the administration of the Society reported in November 1713 that in five years four months Newman

---

[1] Mr. Edward Nicholson at Cumin, near Sligo, Nov. 23rd, 1717. This is one of many examples of Newman's befriending young men.

[2] Nov. 25th, 1725.

had written 6340 letters (all with his own hand, as we have seen), kept the accounts, made abstracts of all inward letters and fair copies of the minutes, copied all important documents, kept records of Charity Schools throughout the country, managed Dr. Bray's Parochial Libraries, and indexed letter and minute books. The Committee recognized his great services by voting a gratuity of £50 and an increase of salary to £80 for the next two years, and then to £100. This, and the special consideration given during his illness, when a gratuity of £10 10s. was voted for convalescence at Hampstead, seemed to Newman very generous, and so he paid out of his own pocket half the clerk's salary of 8s. a week, besides providing him with board and lodging, until in 1727 he asked that 4s. a week be charged to the Society; with some diffidence, " it gives me not a little uneasiness that I cant serve them upon the same terms that their Treasurers do ".[1] His housekeeper cost him £20 12s. a year and her board and he paid the Society £10 a year rent.[2] He had previously written in these terms: " I consider myself and all that I have as the property of the Society and if I save any thing in their service, it is my intention if it please God I dy in it to leave it to them, but if my zeal for their service should carry me so far as to spend more than my income in a frugal way of living, I am not sure they would approve of my running into debt to serve them." [3]

Relations with the Committee were uniformly harmonious throughout the thirty-five years, with two exceptions. In June 1714 a long debate took place, in which the Secretary's conduct was censured. The reason was his continued correspondence with New England friends, who were regarded as sectaries. He had defended himself in a letter of March 9th to Dr. Smalridge, Dean of Christ Church. Many of the New England ministers would take Holy Orders if it were possible " without the hazard of going 1000 leagues ". " Nor am I ashamed to own that I am one of their proselytes . . . the honour I bear to those absent gentlemen who are the glory of their native country for their piety and learning." On another occasion he apologized in a manly way to the Society whom he called " my masters ": " The presumption of yesterday, was meant with all the respect and love as Lord William Powlett's servant lately shew'd to his master when he presumed to take him by the beard when he fell from his horse. Whatever decency was

[1] Dr. Mayo, June 30th, 1727.
[2] The Society paid £44 a year for the rent of the chambers and £10 a year " parish dues ".
[3] Dr. Mayo, Dec. 18th, 1718.

wanting in the manner I am sorry for it and beg you will excuse it." [1]

It is surprising to find that the death of so admirable a Secretary caused no expression of regret to be recorded in the minutes. Three of the Committee reported at the next meeting that they were executors of Newman's will, but no further mention is made of him. Probably the explanation is that formal resolutions of regret were not the fashion, and there were no next of kin in England. [2]

Three of the clerks deserve mention. Mr. Delagarde, presumably a " poor proselyte ", was discharged in 1734. " He was of little more service than as a spectator in the office . . . fickleness and constant application to dramatick amusements dispos'd him to neglect my business." Delagarde was succeeded by Norman, who broke down in 1742, when Newman wrote to the Society to say he could not abandon him after so long and faithful service ; he offered to pay him £5 a year if the Society would do the same. The letter offering the post to a man who had left his employment should be recorded. [3]

> . . . one that writes a masterly running hand like Norman. That will be content to lodge in the office where John did, and can shave and help me with my shoes in a morning and never be absent above $\frac{1}{4}$ of an hour from the office without leave, to be regular in his conduct every Sunday, always attending Divine Service somewhere and to be at home early in the evening. You know the nature of my business and way of life and if you can submit to these and promise never to desert me so abruptly as you did I can bear with the defect of your writing in hopes you will take pains to improve it.
>
> I am,
Sir,
Your very humble servant.

The Newman Letters as a whole leave an impression of reverence for the personality of one's fellowmen, expressed in uniform courtesy to rich and poor alike. The ceremonious approach to the aristocracy was paralleled by the courtesy shown to the lower orders. Indeed the eighteenth century was a period in which the virtue of subordination was compatible with a fundamental democracy.

[1] Mr. Chamberlayn, August 22nd, 1722. An eminent linguist and courtier. Secretary of S.P.C.K. till March 1702. First Secretary of the S.P.G.

[2] Mr. Newman of Wandsworth, who died on July 11th, reputed worth £20,000 (*Gentlemen's Magazine* 1743, p. 389), is not our man.

[3] Mr. Thomson at Edmonton, March 10th, 1743.

III. AMERICAN AFFAIRS

Newman corresponded continually with America : the Governors, especially Jonathan Belcher (Governor of New England 1730–41),[1] the Presidents of Harvard and Yale, the ministers of New England, his relations and old business friends, and the early settlers of Georgia, account for nearly all the letters. There is very little reference to the missionaries sent from England by the S.P.G., for they were the concern of that Society, generally termed by Newman " the Corporation " or " the Corporation Society ".

Newman was appointed agent for the Province of New Hampshire in 1717 and in March 1729 he wrote to suggest a fee of £10 a year for his services, out-of-pocket expenses extra. This from 1717 up to Midsummer 1729 amounted to £120 agency fee plus £77 6s. for disbursements. The work was mainly concerned with a long drawn out boundary dispute between New Hampshire and Massachusetts.[2]

The most interesting of the letters[3] deal with the secular and ecclesiastical politics of New England. Writing to the Rev. Mr. Wadsworth, President of Harvard,[4] Newman sent specimen addresses of loyalty to George II on his accession : " in perusing those from our Universities I could not help thinking it would become our [5] Cantabrigian Mother in America to take this occasion of addressing the Throne. You have as good or perhaps a better title to it than many bodies here that daily do it, as you are a fountain of daring and undissembled loyalty to His Majesty ever praying for perpetual blessings on the illustrious Protestant Succession. . . ." One reason for thus emphasizing loyalty appears in a letter to the Hon. Colonel Quincy :[6] ". . . Nor am I less pleas'd to understand that you are of the number of those worthy patriots who have been in the interest of our country against those who would banish the King's authority, from among them at the same time they must necessarily live under his protection, or cease to be Englishmen, a happiness I hope they will learn to value hereafter if they cannot be persuaded to it now."

[1] The Belcher Papers contain many references to Newman as well as letters to him.
[2] The *Dictionary of American Biography* says he was occasionally employed by New Hampshire from 1709 to 1720. But his letter is explicit.
[3] Some of which are printed in Allen and McClure's History of the S.P.C.K.
[4] July 15th, 1727.
[5] Writing to Americans Newman always identifies himself with them, saying " we ".   [6] Aug. 22nd, 1723.

Perhaps the most interesting letter from the Church standpoint is a very long one to the Rev. Dr. Colman of Boston,[1] printed in the History of the S.P.C.K., which shows the difficulties Newman experienced through his defence of the New Englanders. The concluding part of the letter, which is omitted there, has a bearing on modern controversies.

> If we consider every *Bishop* or *Superintendent* of the Christian Church as a great Presbyter, and every *Presbyter* with a cure of souls regularly ordain'd as a little Bishop . . . it might go a good way towards obviating the invidious distinctions that subsist among us.
>
> But where inveterate customs have establish'd themselves as Episcopacy is with the addition of temporalities blended with the constitution of England and Presbyterianism in Scotland, it would be turning the world upside down to oblige people to alter an establishment that implies no idolatry nor deviation from the fundamentals of Christianity and with which they may go to heaven let them be on which side of the question they please.

Letters to the great Dr. Berkeley, at Rhode Island, and to John Wesley are printed in the S.P.C.K. History, which however omits the interesting postscript to a letter addressed to Berkeley, dated Sept. 17th, 1729.

> I just now receiv'd the enclosed from Lord Perceval and must let you know what the New England men here say of you, that you are so complaisant to the Quakers that you even go to their meetings and preach among 'em and they in their turn go to church, where your dispensation with the use of the surplice and some other observances here particularly the 30th of January etc.[2] would disgust weak people. I tell 'em I believe St. Paul would have done the same if he had been in your place.

Newman bought books for the library at Harvard and for the public library at Portsmouth; also scientific instruments for Yale.[3] He refers to the sending of books to a Mr. Doucett. "I have sent him a few books by a ship that is to sail next Monday to amuse him in the tedious winters of that country, where there is little conversation but with wolves and bears, or about them."

The part played by the S.P.C.K. in the settling of the Salzburg refugees in Georgia deserves a little monograph. All we need do here is to quote passages referring to General Oglethorpe, the leader

---

[1] Sept. 24th, 1736.
[2] Commemoration Service of King Charles' martyrdom.
[3] He acted as intermediary between Americans and the Royal Society in placing their scientific communications.

of the original expedition. After an enthusiastic panegyric on the General [1]—

> I had almost forgot to tell you that Mr. Oglethorpe out of his zeal for the English Plantations has promoted the setting up of a free school for the children of poor planters in America that will come over for education, little knowing how well our forefathers provided for us in New England . . . [A site and some money have been obtained] . . . This is well meant, but Mr. Oglethorpe will I hope be convinc'd when he sees our Colleges at Cambridge that his school had better be on the Common in their neighbourhood.

It is a remarkable piece of self denial that such a man as Mr. Oglethorpe should renounce the amenities of life in England. [2]

> . . . should cross a perilous ocean for the sake of establishing a few distressed families undone by idleness, intemperance, sickness or other ill habits oppress'd and all with poverty, to found a colony in a wilderness wholly uncultivated, abounding with pine barrens, crocodiles, bears and wolves with other animals of no apparent use to the creation, but to punish the posterity of fallen Adam. This is not to be accounted for by narrow souls because it does not yeild of any immediate visible reward but the distant expectation of an uncertain glory like what Julius Caesar enjoy'd when he landed in Britain about 1700 years ago with a more promising people than are now the first planters of Georgia . . .

Here is a letter to the Hon. James Oglethorpe, Esq., at Savannah in Georgia, June 4th, 1736.

> . . . America is much beholden to gentlemen of your genius, for without such, the aboriginal natives, and their children might have slept on to the end of the world, and never heard of any other way of living than in wigwams, or one remove from the wild beasts of the forest. I hope the examples which the Europeans under your discipline will set to the natives, will give virtue an aimiable lustre, and let them see that the Christian religion is not only in name but in reality an improvement of the divine and social virtues which adorn the humane species.
>
> I own it is easier to speculate upon things of this kind than to put them in practice, but I hope you are the *White-man* that will, according to the tradition of the Indians, deliver them from the darkness that has for many ages spread over them.

Lastly, in 1742 Newman, having tried to find boys for Oglethorpe, wrote to say that he had been to all the chief schools in and around London. "Where I had a choice of 700 or 800 boys and found

---

[1] A letter to His Excellency Governor Belcher, Nov. 6th, 1732.
[2] Letter to Mr. John Vat at Ebenezer in Georgia, Oct. 10th, 1735.

D

several willing to accept of your service but they were either of a dwarfed stature, hump back'd, squint ey'd, or bandy leg'd, and most destitute of the main qualifications you desired." The parents of the only possible boy refused to let him go.

IV. POLITICAL AND SOCIAL MATTERS

As this is not intended as a historical study, it seems best to give Newman's views without comment, with a warning that they must be checked by the standard histories of the period. In 1712 Marlborough had fallen and the stage was set for the struggle inevitably impending when Queen Anne died. Civil war seemed more than a possibility. Newman wrote to The Hague.[1]

> . . . Popish preists come daily over to us from Dunkirk to pave the way for some design which they seem to be big of, and there are already many instances of perversion to their bloody religion which shew that they are not idle, but God will I hope frustrate all their devices tho' when I consider the prevalence of our impietys and that more than 50 thousand righteous souls have not by their intercessions been able to save the Kingdom of France from the plagues that have visited it, what can we expect but to be given up to the destruction we have deserved and to be involv'd in the ruin which impends us till the wise purposes of God are accomplish'd.

Queen Anne died on Aug. 1st, 1714, and George I was proclaimed. On Aug. 27th Newman wrote again to Mr. Hales.

> . . . I can't help repeating my congratulations for the happy turn these Kingdoms seem to have taken in so short a time as His Majesty has reign'd. It is not to be imagined what a silence has overspread our party prize-fighters so that whereas about a month since a pamphlet warr rag'd with that vehemence that some even dar'd to give odious insinuations of the most august family of Hanover, we are now in such a profound tranquility as one would have thought impossible could have succeeded so soon the unnatural ferment we were in. The choice of the Regency is an earnest of that wisdom with which His Majesty is endow'd, and their resolves hitherto have convinc'd His Majesty's subjects that they study the honour of His Majesty and the welfare of his people. It is not a month since men dar'd publickly to avow the interests of the Pretender as if they were sure to be supported when ever his title should be in question, but now he is spoke of with as much contempt as a spurious creature ought to be and one would think that either his advocates were vanish'd or had chang'd their minds, I question much the latter but am told ship loads of 'em go over daily to France to tell their Master that the game is irretrievably lost, for the bias of the nation to the House of Hanover upon the King's being proclaim'd

[1] Mr. Hales, Nov. 25th, 1712

was so great that it would have been downright madness for any to have made the least opposition. . . . It must be own'd that the councils of men have not wrought this change but the allpowerful hand of God has so wonderfully disposed things at a critical juncture when all was give for lost, and some bishops in the country expected to have the crown of martyrdom, all their fears are at once dispell'd and we are as happy as the people that wake out of a frightfull dream . . .

On September 24th he wrote again to Mr. Hales, now at Hanover, describing the arrival of the King and the Prince.

At least a thousand boats and barges went down to meet him. At Graves End the Mayor and Aldermen went on board in their formalities with a very loyal address and had the honour to kiss his Majesty's and the Prince's hands, as they advanced up with the tyde the King being now in his own barge and the Prince in another royal barge it was the most beautifull scene in the world to see so many watermen pulling with their oars with the same eagerness as men running a race, filling the river with foam and the air with shouts . . .

Guns were fired at Woolwich and Blackwall. The Prince landed first at Greenwich and was embraced by the Duke of Marlborough and other great officers. Then the King landed and the great men went down on their knees. Signals given from Greenwich Hospital set the batteries firing . . .

While the guns at the Tower and in the river near London roar'd like thunder at a distance and serv'd as a bass note to this royal musick which with the acclamations of about 30 or 40 thousand people and all the drums and trumpets of Guards made the most glorious noise that ever I heard in my life. It is impossible to express the joy that was to be seen in people's countenances on this occasion, every one being ready to leap out of his skin. The witty Dr. Garth standing by my Lord Chief Justice Parker (one of the Regency) said to him, *I am glad your Excellency is depos'd*. Soon after the King landed it grew dark and all Nature seem'd to be illuminated with bonfires skyrockets and candles ; I return'd that night to London and had the pleasure to see the ships illuminated with lanthorns and every garret window and alley even in Wapping and Southwark garnish'd with candles so that you might have seen to read there as at noonday.

The next day was Sunday and, though travel by the river was forbidden, " all mankind " went to Greenwich by water or land to see the King.

The royal entry was the next day being Monday the 20th current perform'd in so magnificent a manner that I want words to describe it. You may perhaps guess at it by conceiving of above 200 coaches and six dressed up in ribbons of all colours belonging to the nobility and gentry who presented themselves that morning at Greenwich and according to the ceremonial which no doubt you have seen in print the procession began about 12 o'clock from Greenwich. At St. Margaret's Hill in Southwark the Lord Mayor and Aldermen and Recorder of London on horseback met the King and the Recorder made a speech to him in the name of the City, then the City Sword being presented to His Majesty by the Lord Mayor on his knees he was pleased to return it to him who bore it before the King bear headed to St. James's. I can't give you an idea of the spectators equal to what it really was, but you may imagine how it would appear if one continued gallery were built on each sides of the street from the Monument to Charing Cross 4, 6, 8, and sometimes 10 seats deep, and all crowded with people in their best apparel, but then you must add to it, every chamber and garret window full of heads the carnishes [cornices] and ledges on the outside of the houses and even the sign posts hung with people like caterpillars ; In short if all England had been there a greater appearance could not have been made because there was no room to receive them. . . . The procession extended about 3 mile computing the cavalcade and coaches . . . tho' His Majesty set out from Greenwich about noon, it was past 7 before he reach'd to St. James's. The Charity Children made a goodly appearance in St. Paul's Churchyard which the King and Prince were extreamly pleas'd with, so that His Highness said he never saw any thing so fine, and that he only wish'd he had had his own children with him to see 'em at the same time.

The second George aroused equal enthusiasm.[1]

The news of our late gracious King's death [2] you will believe was very surprizing which for a time gave a damp to all our towering hopes built on the success of His Majesty's wise administration, but in a few days the overflow of joy that has run thro' these Kingdoms on the peacefull occasion of our present gracious Sovereign has dry'd up all our tears while George I reigns in George II with this difference that His present Majesty has some advantages that his father wanted as youthfull vigour, the English language and long application to the study of our constitution so that those who through an obstinate humour could not bring themselves to submit to the father, seeing all their views of distressing their country at an end now gladly lay hold of the opportunity of making their court to the son as if he had some excellencies or right which the father had not, though in truth all the difference is in themselves whose eyes are open'd. . . .

Just now the King and Queen attended with their Courts in the royal barges and a vast concourse of boats are passing by the Temple on the river while the air is rended with acclamations at so glorious a sight. . . . In short this nation by a series of miracles seems to be the darling of heaven as much as ever the children of Israel were. . . .

The Coronation was not long delayed.[3]

The preparation for the Coronation is beyond expression for riches and magnificence; the quality that can't afford to buy jewels hire 'em

[1] Letter to the Rev. Mr. President Wadsworth at Harvard College, July 15th, 1727.   [2] June 10th, 1727.
[3] Jonathan Belcher, at Boston, Oct. 2nd, 1727.

at 5£ per cent for the use of 'em to give splendor to the ceremony of that day. The Queen's robes on that day are estimated at a million of money sterling, nay I am told that Her Majesty's petticoat is so loaded with jewels that, that alone will be worth the money. . . .

Newman, who went to Court sometimes, was able to advise others.[1]

. . . When you go on the errand you propose, you have only to take your opportunity any morning and ask for the Lord of the Bedchamber in waiting, to whom it will be necessary to present a copy of your book, that he may be the better able to speak to it when he presents you to the King. Sunday is not a proper time, because it is a publick day attended with a great crowd, and Thursday is much like it, but if you attend any other day soon after 12 you will be in time.

When war broke out in 1740 after a long interval of peace London had experienced a very severe winter with much unemployment. Coal was three guineas a chaldron and hard to get because of ice in the river.[2] By 1742 suffering was acute : " the present taxes for the poor in some places with the 4s. in the pound paid to the King reduces a man of 200£ p.a. to 100£ ".[3]

. . . The success of Admiral Vernon at Carthagena, the news of which has fill'd the town with more noise and illuminations than ever I knew upon any occasion because it held 2 nights together to oblige the mob it being holiday time ; I shew'd lights the first night, but because I did not the 2nd my neighbours and I that omitted that respect to 'em had our windows broke.

An interesting letter in defence of the Charity Schools, which were attacked for making servants hard to get, shows Newman in advance of his time.[4]

It is not to be wonder'd at, that a footman or a postillion's place should be fill'd with more difficulty when 30 thousand of the dreggs of the nation it might be said 4 times that number since the first in-stitution of Charity Schools are drawn into a life of better views, for these creatures were heretofore the desease of the nation as they are still in France, and in all countries where oppression and poverty reigns. And those that will have 4 footmen and a postillion to attend 'em whenever they go abroad I hope may be enabled by the growing wealth of the nation to send to France and Germany for 'em when they can no longer find any in England that will devote themselves to so insipid a life. Every waterman's boy stands fairer to serve his country more usefully than any Duke's footman in the Kingdom that is capable of

[1] Letter to Mr. Zach. Williams at No. 4 in the Charterhouse, Dec. 6th, 1739.
[2] Letter of Jan. 29th, 1740.
[3] April 3rd, 1742.
[4] John Chamberlayne, Dec. 15th, 1722.

nothing else: The rise of wages is a consequence of wealth and that the children do find better business than being footmen, which is a comfortable omen to the Kingdom. . . .

After the nation has tyr'd it self with fruitless pursuits of riches in South Sea Bubbles etc. it seems now to be returning to the old certain way of acquiring wealth by industry and frugality. . . .

A description of a popular resort is given in a letter to a lady.[1]

I have inform'd my self of the character of the entertainments at Marybone, and find them resemble those at Vauxhall as much as a well order'd ale house with Delf ware and lattice work does a good tavern with china and fine paintings. Some of the violins there are from Vauxhall, the trumpets and kettle drums are good tho' not from Vauxhall whence the best trumpet I am told is gone to Cupper's Garden. The company at Marybone is not half so much as at Vauxhall seldom above 300 or 400 in an evening, and rarely any quality among them. Their terms of admittance and for eatables and drinkables in the evening are the same as at Vauxhall. But I am told they make the most of their company at breakfast there in the morning when they give nothing to be admitted but pay 1s. for the coffee and tea they drink and 18d. if they have chocolate. But they have no music in the morning except the French horn.

In the evening every one pays a shilling for admittance and eats and drinks, or not, as he pleases as they do at Vauxhall. There is a grotto in the neighbourhood which they say is worth seeing and that 1s. is given to see the shell work of it. I believe you will think the curiosities there hardly worth spending a night in town to see but if you are inclin'd to spend some morning there you will see every thing worth seeing and guess at the rest.

On the whole the eighteenth century looks attractive in these letters. To help to give a balanced view, these extracts may be useful. Newman writes to Mr. Chamberlain [2] to say that the chaplain of the Marshalsea prison assures him that at least 200 persons imprisoned for debt have died of starvation in a year. Will Mr. Chamberlain take up the matter with Members of Parliament? "If this enquiry were extended to all the prisons in the Kingdom . . . I believe it would disclose such a scene of cruelty as is not to be equalized in Turkey nor in Barbary itself."

Writing to Col. Drysdale, Governor of Virginia, Newman says: [3]

Counsellor Layer after being repreiv'd several times for about 5 months past that the Lords as well as the Commons might sift him and also to give him an opportunity of meriting his pardon by making discoverence was yesterday executed at Tyburn, and his head was this

---

[1] Mrs. Forman, June 6th, 1740.
[2] June 9th, 1715. The name is spelled variously.
[3] May 18th, 1723.

morning set up at Temple Barr, his quarters being given to his relations by the indulgence of the Government. While his bowels were on the coals some of the mobb scambled for his heart etc. and the black guard boys took that occasion to retale his entrails, and 2d. was given for a peice of his liver as big as a pea, which I suppose was first got at some butcher's shambles.

V. DEALINGS WITH AUTHORS

Publishing in anything like the modern sense of the term took very little of the Secretary's time. The method adopted was to acquire the right to publish pamphlets and small books which had proved their worth. A number of early assignments of such works by the printer Downing to the Society are preserved. A few letters deserve to be quoted. In 1713 Newman wrote to Steele recommending a manuscript for *The Guardian*. The advice which follows is as apposite today as when it was first given.[1]

> . . . Give me leave now my hand is in to shoot another bolt, I remember to have read it somewhere that if an author will suffer his composition to lie by him a year or more and then peruse it it will come forth with more advantage and he will not repent the delay of its publication ; since it is in obedience to your command of being as ill natured as possible, I depend on your goodness to indulge this impertinence.

If a publisher might write such a letter today with phraseology suitably changed, an author would be much surprised to receive one like this.[2]

> Thank you for the Essays in Poetry which accompany'd your last ; I am very unfit to criticize on them or any performance of that nature, only give me leave to observe what my Lord and Mr. Chamberlayne both agreed in (for I shew'd them to none else) that as you propose God willing to devote your self to theological studies, you would find your account in it to be deaf and blind to Bellinda's charms, the contemplation of which will never yeild an establish'd tranquility to the mind, but instead of it may perhaps give a biass which may cost many a struggle to conquer. This 'tis very probable was one of the reasons why a learn'd prelate of our Church, when any person apply'd to him for Holy Orders, the first question he ask'd him, was, whether he was a poet ? And if he answer'd in the affirmative, the Bishop told him he would have nothing to do with him, for fear of bringing an unprofitable labourer into God's vineyard. Perhaps his Lordship was so severe, being conscious to himself of having spent many hours in his younger days, to print luscious ideas on his mind by these kind of exercises, instead of those diviner amusements which would have been more suitable to the business and character he afterwards sustain'd.

[1] Whitelock Bulstrode, Dec. 7th, 1720.
[2] Mr. Barrett at Ashted in Surrey, Oct. 30th, 1722.

Even more discouraging was a letter of 1723 to the Rev. Mr. Galpine, chaplain to the Duke of Portland, Governor of Jamaica, who had sent a sermon to be printed.

> The sermon was twice as long as the sermons usually are here and therefore the charge double tho' managed with all the frugality possible. Pray how can you afford in respect to your health and your hearers to make such long sermons in such a hot country, if you commonly practise it, it must be a great prejudice to your health if not disgusting to your auditors.

Though Newman had little opportunity of showing his literary gifts, if any, except by the forceful English of his letters, that he appreciated literature is proved by this remarkable letter to the Secretary of the Lord Chancellor.[1]

> I hear the daughter of the famous Milton is in great straights, several of her scholars having left her, and others not been able to pay her for their schooling. If my Lord Chancellor knew her case I am persuaded His Lordship would find means to procure a small pension of 20 or 25 £ per annum from the Government which would make the remainder of her life easie, nor could it be thought a burthen on the Government considering she is (as I think) turned of 70.[2] Pray make her case known to Sir Richard Blackmore who wants neither inclination nor interest to procure some relief for her. It would be a great reproach to our time to let such a person suffer for want of the common necessaries of life, whose very raggs would be sacred relics 100 years hence in the opinion of a true admirer of her incomparable father. I shall with pleasure show you the way to her cell, whenever you think fit to command.

VI. Other Interests

Under this head I have collected a number of things which do not obviously belong to the previous sections.

A book printer takes an apprentice for seven years on payment of £35; no charges in respect of clothes, washing, or sickness to be the master's liability (March 13th, 1740). "The bearer James Davies is an honest mustard maker and heartily well affected to King George. If you can recommend him to serve His Majesty's kitchen with mustard, I dare say when his goods are try'd he will need no further recommendation" (Mr. Salter, James Street, Aug. 4th, 1718). A letter of March 16th, 1714, to Mr. Samuel Palmer at Tauris, Merchant in Turkey, accompanies a map of Persia. Will he

---

[1] Mr. Hughes, Dec. 29th, 1718.
[2] Mary Milton, born 1648, who never married, would have been just under 70 at this date.

return it with comments and corrections? Is there anything in those parts which will help to elucidate Scripture? Is there any evidence of the lost ten tribes or of the Deluge? Professor Francke was one of the original Professors of the pietist University of Halle. Writing to him on May 28th, 1719,[1] Newman penned a panegyric of Germany, which on second thoughts he crossed out.

> While I write this, casting my eye on a mapp of the world, I could not help observing that Germany is near the centre of the extreams of the known habitable parts of our globe, and consequently by her situation the fittest country to invigorate the most distant nations with the most important truths. And as Hall is near the centre of Germany her situation with the vast accession of learning and other emoluments which Providence has graciously vouchsafed does not less adapt her to be the primum mobile of all intelligence for the improvement of mankind.

Letters to the Governor of the Bahamas and to the Marquis Du Quesne in Jamaica tell the recipients not to send commodities as presents; it is cheaper to buy them than to get them out of the Custom House.

Two letters show the embarrassment caused by another kind of present. (To My Lord Perceval, Sept. 30th, 1727.)

> I have lately had a present of a little innocent black boy native of Jamaica, a beauty of his kind, but as my circumstances don't require or admit of such a servant the best use I can make of him is to present him to such a patron as your Lordship to whom I am under so many and great obligations, and if your Lordship will vouchsafe to accept of him to wait on you My Lady and your children I shall hope to see him become a good Christian and a faithful servant. He is not yet christen'd but if he has the honour to serve your Lordship I am sure he wont want that priviledge long. I should not presume to make this tender, if he was not a boy of so promising a genius, that I have reason to think if God spare his life he will prove a dutifull servant. . . .

(To the Bishop of London, Oct. 12th, 1727.)

> Having a present made to me of a good natured little black boy native of Jamaica a beauty of his kind but not christen'd I have accepted of him upon condition I may have leave to make a present of him to your Lordship in acknowledgment of your great tenderness to the souls of the whole race of Negroes.
> If I have such leave by the bearer or otherwise, he shall be deliver'd at Whitehall or Fulham free of any charge to your Lordship. . . .

On another occasion Newman received a present of two live wild geese, which he sent to the Bishop at once.

[1] Writing to a foreigner, Newman adds " O.S ".

He wrote to the Bishop of St. Asaph to thank for sermons (Oct. 9th, 1711).

> There is no good man in the plantations but must subscribe to your Lordship's sentiments, and when it pleases God to give the Society possession of their estates at Barbados I hope their example will shame others into a Christian treatment of their slaves, I had almost said Turkish treatment, for the Mahometans to encourage proselytes give 'em their freedom absolutely, but that may be a degree of humanity which our heathenish Christians cannot come up to.

He tells Mr. Robert Hales (at the Cockpit, Whitehall, March 4th, 1718) that ladies are the best to raise money for the " Black Guard School "—" they ask in so powerful a manner that they'll get 100 guineas in the time that men would get 20 ".

An interesting letter to the Rev. Dr. Waterland, Master of Magdalene College, Cambridge [1] (July 5th, 1735), says that the S.P.C.K. has been urging the introduction of Christian authors into Grammar Schools and the laying aside the reading of heathen authors " that are more remarkably profane, lewd, and scandalous ". A long list of books is given, including Minucius Felix, St. Cyprian on the Lord's Prayer, Prudentius, Clement of Rome, Polycarp, Justin Martyr's Apology, and selections from Erasmus, Grotius de Veritate, and " The Whole Duty of Man in elegant Latin ". " The Society hope by the gracious assistance of the Holy Spirit, they shall be enabled to do what shall be most conducive to promote the glory of the pure heavenly religion of our dear crucified Redeemer Christ Jesus, and the salvation of a multitude of souls."

The American Dictionary speaks of Newman's " deep but unobtrusive piety, his broad tolerance, and his joy in giving himself for the welfare of others ". That is well said, but it misses the rarely attractive flavour of his personality, which can best be described by quoting two letters, the one severe, the other tender, but both pastoral-hearted.

The first is written to the Rev. Robert Watts of Great Gidding (the year is not given).

> Give me leave to admonish you for your impatience signify'd in your 2 last letters. If Providence has cast your lot among a perverse people to learn resignation to the Divine Will, meekness under affronts, patience to endure contradiction, in order to qualify you for a greater trust, I'm sorry to find you so averse to profit by those lessons, the want

---

[1] The famous theologian.

of which perhaps may be one great reason why you are detain'd as it were a prisoner in such disagreable company. I cannot imagine how the people refusing so small an expense as 50 shillings towards fitting up a school room for the Charity Children must necessarily put you upon destroying your self. If you have by a pragmatical domineering conduct (pardon the expressions for I can't help considering your case in such a light from your own letters) laboured to extort the benevolence of your neighbours in a matter wherein they are intirely free to do, or not to do according as they were inclin'd, consider whether you have not industriously brought upon your self the contradictions you groan under.

There are many good men in the world that next to the grace of God ow their virtues, and even their preferment to some such afflictions as you complain of: a scolding wife, imperious parents, undutifull children, morose and spitefull neighbours are all blessings to the man that considers 'em as chastisements from heaven, to refine his nature, and to adorn him with the graces of an angel, who has the art of circum-spection so well as they that are liable to be insulted for every frailty: If a man is too loquacious he soon finds his mistake and grows as calm as a lamb among a verbose noisy people: If a man has too high an opinion of his own parts, and ability to govern all mankind if they would but tamely lie at his feet, where is he so likely to acquire a just sense of his weakness on these accounts as among a froward and contra-dictious generation of men.

Dear Sir compose your self to trust in God, be content to make short sermons, and to write short letters, and let your conversation be as edifying and as concise as possible; when you have gain'd these points over your self depend upon it, you will be contented to accept of a translation to a more agreable living. I took the freedom to say something to this effect some months since, but you would not believe
Dear Sir, your most faithfull humble servant.

The other letter is to a young lady who has asked his help to get a post at Court (Mrs., i.e. Miss, Elizabeth Sheldon, Stroud, Gloucester-shire, Aug. 31st, 1727).

. . . In the meantime I have consulted Mr. Hales as you desir'd on the subject of your letter and he told me it was the hardest thing in the world to get any place at Court worth your acceptance, there being few only that belong to the fair sex comparatively but what are engross'd by people of quality for their dependants and to use his own words he told me it was easier to get 10 men into places at Court than one woman.

But I beseech you dont let this discourage you in your happy re-tirement from the envious intrigues and flattering vanities of a Court, which appear glittering to those at a distance but in reality mock those that enjoy them so much, that I'm perswaded there are many of the more thinking Courtiers that would gladly renounce some of the profits of their stations for such a pleasing retreat as you now enjoy. It is justly observ'd by moralists that our lots in life are assign'd to us by heaven but the happiness or unhappiness of those lots very much depends on our selves, on our contentedness and resignation to the will of God who knows what is best for us and out of tenderness as a Father places us in life so as to secure us from the temptations we are most liable to. I see daily the goodness of God in denying me riches etc. for had I half the wealth of some men, I have reason to believe without a miracle of Divine assistance I should be a most extravagant immoral fop, than which I think to be a usefull chimney sweeper or employ'd in the lowest offices is infinitely more preferable.

I know some marry'd couples so unhappy by giving way to inclinations they ought to curb that though they ride in their chariots whenever they please they are miserable whether they are in town or country. The husband places all his happiness in country sports dagling up to the knees in dew with a gun upon his shoulder follow'd by a setting dog in chase of a poor partridge. The lady is never easie but when she is dress'd in brockades rolling in her chariot at the Ring or to the opera. In other instances the husband's heart is in town where he finds greater variety of pleasures to rove in, while his lady finding her self neglected at home longs for the day of their return into the country where she may enjoy more of her husband and 1000 pretty amusements which cant be had in town. . . .

This Madam you may say is foreign to yours and my case who are single, but you will find it exactly parralel when you consider that as they ought to make a virtue of necessity, so we in our stations should do. There is something analogous to husbands wives and children in our way of life. For my own part as Providence has deny'd me the happiness of a wife I endeavour to love my masters and my business as other men do their wives. The Charity Children throughout the Kingdom and my canary birds with my cat and her kitten at home supply the place of children as they engross so much of my time to take care of them, and while it pleases God to give me health and the use of my limbs, I walking a foot envy no man that rides in his chariot and wants that priviledge to compensate for the gout or some other infirmity which I thank God I am a stranger to.

I haven't the happiness of knowing Stroud, but if it were 10 times wilder than any place I ever yet saw at Newfoundland which claims the preference in respect of wildness of all places I'm sure Mrs. Sheldon with her fine genius and education may be happy in it, while she can have a good book to converse with, a happiness that many country people know nothing of, and yet think themselves happy if their poultry, butter and cheese and garden amusements answer their expectation, but you enjoy 'em all and seem not to know it, by wishing your self at Court, the most dangerous state of life in the world.

I own I go thither sometimes because I love the Royal Family, but since I could reflect with judgment I never do go, but I bless my self that my lot is not to live among them, that I am a spectator at liberty and not a trainbearer or some other fine thing confin'd to a place abounding with vanity and insincerity. How many there clad in rich brocade and velvet groan under the burthen of their servile attendance so that they would gladly exchange 2 months of their residence there for one month of the plain happy rural retirement you enjoy. . . .

Perhaps the moralizing is rather conventional, but it is charming. In the next chapter we shall see how Newman tackled the domestic cares from which a bachelor is generally exempt.

III

HENRY NEWMAN AND THE DU QUESNES

IN 1932 Mr. John Beresford published a charming little book entitled *Mr. Du Quesne*, in which he investigated the history of the Rev. Thomas Roger Du Quesne, who held the livings of Honingham and East Tuddenham, in Norfolk, from 1763 to his death in 1793, and is frequently mentioned in Parson Woodforde's Diary. The piquancy of the story lies in the contrast between the swashbuckling Huguenot ancestor, whose portrait looked down on some of the famous dinners described by the Diary, and the calm of the Norfolk village.

Du Quesne's great-grandfather was Admiral Du Quesne (1610–88), who was at sea for sixty years, and was made a Marquis for his services. Henry the eldest son went to live in Switzerland at the revocation of the Edict of Nantes in 1685, and died at Geneva in 1722. The second Marquis had two sons, Gabriel and Marc-Antoine-Jacob; also a daughter. Gabriel, born in Paris about 1684, became a student in philosophy at the University of Geneva in 1699, when the French biographer of the family loses sight of him. In 1709 he was appointed Envoy of the Protestant Cantons to the States General, and came to England to petition Queen Anne on behalf of the Protestants of France. He was naturalized in 1711, entered the Guards in 1712, and in 1717 became Lieut.-Colonel of the 1st Troop of the Grenadier Guards. Later he went to Jamaica as Governor of Port Royal, under the Duke of Portland, without salary or reward, and " it seems that he was superseded in his employment on account of the death of his patron the Duke ". This last piece of information Mr. Beresford got from an unsuccessful petition presented to the Lords of the Treasury in 1740. Du Quesne, now the third Marquis, says that he lost a considerable fortune in 1720 in the South Sea Scheme; a pension was granted him, but George I died in 1727 before it operated, and nothing was done; he is now starving.

The Marquis married Elizabeth, daughter of Sir Roger Bradshaigh, Baronet, and widow of Job Yates. Two children are known to have been born of the marriage: Thomas, baptized at Twickenham on August 28th, 1718, who went to Eton as a scholar in 1729, became a scholar of King's College, Cambridge, in 1738, and Fellow in 1741;

and a daughter, name unknown. Thomas, who never married, in later life held, besides his two livings, the offices of Prebendary of Lichfield, Rector of Scole, Chancellor Canon of St. David's, and Prebendary of Ely. In a remarkable will, now in the possession of Miss Du Cane,[1] he left money to the Powells and W. Burden, poor relations, descendants of his sister, who married a Mr. French.

Such in brief is Mr. Beresford's story. The archives of the S.P.C.K. contain a series of letters which correct and amplify it.

Henry Newman, Secretary of the Society 1708-43, was a devoted friend of the family who, by what was a stroke of good fortune for us, wrote his private letters from his office, so that the drafts, from which the actual letters were copied by his clerk, are still extant. I am not familiar with the social history of the time and cannot say whether they are as unique in their charm as they seem to me coming to them with fresh eyes. But they are indispensable to the reconstruction of Newman's character and provide valuable evidence to show how, 200 years ago, a bachelor dealt with the problem of a spendthrift father, and children who had to be clothed and educated.

First let me correct Mr. Beresford's facts. There were five children : Ann, William, Thomas, Elizabeth, and Henry (the probable order). The Marquis' post in Jamaica was well paid, and he lost it through misconduct.

The S.P.C.K. story begins in 1719 with a letter to Sir Thomas Lowther, of Holker, dated Sept. 24th.[2] The Marquis Du Quesne and his lady with their son have returned from Paris, having left the little girl with the old Marquis at Geneva ; " the Marquis brought home with him a flux which he attributes to his eating too many of the tempting grapes of the country ". (The daughter is Ann, the son William, born Jan. 11th, 1716.) In 1721 the Duke of Portland is appointed Governor of Jamaica. Newman tells him that Colonel Rogers, late Governor of the Bahamas, will give him an account of the West Indies (Sept. 20th) and describes the politics of Jamaica, where the Country party and the Court party divide the field, the former being the stronger, though the latter has more influence in England (Oct. 29th). He takes Du Quesne to see the

---

[1] Of Fittleworth House, Sussex, who has provided me with some information about the Du Cane branch of the family.

[2] The addressees and the dates of the letters are henceforward generally given in the notes. The punctuation and spelling of the drafts are followed, but not the rather erratic use of capitals. Abbreviations evidently intended to be written out in full by the clerk are not followed. All the dates derived from the letters are " old style ", without adjustment to the true date, as in Chapter II.

Duke and arranges for Mrs. (i.e. Miss) Mary Jackson to travel with Lady Du Quesne as her gentlewoman.

" My Lady Torrington ", Ann's godmother and the generous friend of the family, first appears in a letter of June 8th, 1722. There were four women bearing this title during our period. The Earl of Torrington (Herbert) died in 1716 and his widow in 1719. Viscount Torrington (Byng, ancestor of the present holder of the title), who died in 1733, had eleven sons and four daughters, so his wife (died in 1756) cannot be our Lady Torrington, who is described as childless. Nor can the wife of his son, the second Viscount, though she left no issue, her three children having died young, for " My Lady Torrington " comes in the letters long before her husband succeeded to the title. We are left with the wife of Baron Torrington, created 1716, died 1719, second son of the first Earl of Bradford; she was Anne, second daughter of Robert Pierrepoint of Nottingham, and died in February 1735.[1]

In June 1722 Lady Du Quesne, who was waiting at Portsmouth for the ship to sail, went, by permission of the Duke, to see her child Elizabeth, who was dangerously ill, and Lady Torrington.[2] The children were left behind, including Harry, the baby, whose parents " left him to my care ". Only for a few weeks, however, for presently Newman wrote: " I have never parted with a child with more regret than with him, for though he could not speak every feature in his face made a thousand orations for him, and his incessant good humour oblig'd every body that play'd with him to love him." [3] The two boys, Billy and Tommy, were left at a kind of nursery school kept by the Rev. Mr. Lefevre and his wife at Church Lane, Chelsea, French refugees. The fees for the two were £64 a year, clothes extra. This comes from a letter to Mr. Jacob Montross, brother of the Marquis, who was living at Southampton to perfect his English.[4]

On Oct. 14th Newman went to Eton to see the Duke's sons, the Marquis of Titchfield and Lord George; he reported on their health in a letter of the 17th to the Duke, adding on the 20th a hope that the Duke and Duchess, and the Ladies Ann and Belle, have arrived happily. On Nov. 12th he wrote to the Marquis to

[1] I am indebted to Sir Gerald Wollaston, Garter King of Arms, for enabling me to interpret the evidence of The Complete Peerage.
[2] Lady Torrington, June 28th.
[3] The Revd. Mr. Galpine, chaplain to the Duke, Oct. 20th, 1722.
[4] Sept. 25th, 1722. In later letters he is often called Mr. Du Quesne Montross; or Mr. Du Quesne. I cannot explain the name Montross; perhaps he had married an heiress and taken her name.

announce the death of Elizabeth on Oct. 21st; to inform him that he has had no success in the Dutch lotteries; and to say he has been to see the children at Chelsea. "I heard Billy say his prayers and his lesson in French." In the same month the old Marquis died at Geneva and his widow sent for her son Jacob, who set out at the end of the year, after dining in company with Newman with Lady Torrington at her house in New Bond Street.[1] Newman says of the boys: "Their cloaths being thin I have put them in mourning for their grandpapa in a dark grey drugget trim'd with black."[2] A little later he went to see the children and gave them twenty kisses from their mother. When giving this information he added a copy of Ann's first letter to her godmother Lady Torrington, from Geneva.[3]

> Madam,
> I should be guilty if I did not offer to your Ladyship the beginning of my writing. I beg of your Ladyship to pardon me that liberty, to accept of my humble duty, as from one who shall endeavour to be worthy your benevolence by being with the greatest respect,
> Madam,
Your Ladyship's obedient servant
Ann Du Quesne.

It will be convenient to tell the story of the Duke first. He was voted a salary of £5000 a year, twice as much as the previous Governor.[4] Newman refers [5] to the Duke's desire to improve the morals of the island, "which has hithertoo been look'd on as the most abandon'd of the King's Dominions to all sorts of wickedness. . . . Fanaticism cant and hypocrisy are justly odious everywhere yet these names are often unjustly used to ridicule any approach to virtue where vice has got the ascendant, but your Grace's high character puts you out of the reach of any such imputations." We find Newman suggesting that the Duke should set up Charity Schools, telling him of the wonderful effects of the new Whitehall Preachers on the loyalty of the clergy,[6] and enclosing a letter from the Bishop of London.[7] The Duke died in Jamaica on July 4th, 1726.[8] Mistakes caused by

---

[1] Her other addresses were Twickenham and occasionally Bath.
[2] Marquis Du Quesne, Jan. 5th, 1723.
[3] Marquis Du Quesne, Feb. 18th, 1723.
[4] Marquis Du Quesne, April 20th, 1723.
[5] Duke of Portland, July 31st, 1723.
[6] Part of the policy concerted by the Bishop of London (Gibson) and the Whig Government, to wean the clergy from Jacobitism.
[7] Duke of Portland, Aug. 24th, 1723.
[8] Not 1724 as given in *The Complete Peerage* (old edition), evidently by error, for Newman's letters to the Duke continued through 1725 and 1726.

E

following Du Quesne's advice would have led to his recall had he lived. The body was brought home to England and " was last night interr'd, with great pomp, from the Jerusalem Chamber, in Henry VII's Chappel ".[1]

Earlier letters tell of visits to the Duke's sons. Having met Colonel Shute, Governor of New England, at Court, he took him to Eton to see them. " The Marquis retains his gravity with a manly thoughtfullness, and Lord George is so spritly that he grudges every minute that is not spent in some violent exercise, and if it were safe for him to jump from a precipice as high as St. Pauls he would be glad to do it, to outrun those voluble spirits that incessantly urge him to perpetual motion. As opposite as they seem to be in temper, they are exceeding fond of each other; the Marquis put on the gravity of an indulgent father, and Lord George caresses him with the regards of a son, whenever his brother commends or admonishes him." [2] Newman took the little Du Quesnes to see them. He reported that Lord George has danced with Princess Anne; he performs on the musket, drilled by the Marquis, for Newman's benefit; he is in the habit of drilling with the Grenadier Guards in the Park. The elder boy, Marquis of Titchfield, became the second Duke of the Bentinck line in 1726. It is pleasant to learn from *The Complete Peerage* that he grew up to be, according to Hearne, " reported to be the handsomest man in England ", and that he married Lady Margaret Cavendish, daughter of the second Earl of Oxford, Prior's " my noble, lovely, little Peggy ". He died in 1762 and was buried in Westminster Abbey.

Lady Du Quesne must have lived for the mail, having such a correspondent as Newman. But " The less you suffer my Lady Du Quesne to live in sight of the ocean or ships the easier she will be in her mind, that she may not think of letters till they come ". He recalls his own experience of scanning the sea for ships when he lived in America.[3]

The letters throw interesting side-lights on economic conditions. Newman has been asked to find workmen and clerks. Carpenters and bricklayers insist on wages of £20 to £40 a year with all found, a quarter paid in advance in England; 5s. a week while waiting for a ship, and £7 for passage money. A bricklayer refuses these terms and £30 a year. Christ's Hospital is the best place to look for a clerk.

[1] Westminster Abbey. Marquis Du Quesne, Nov. 4th, 1726.
[2] Duke of Portland, Aug. 31st, 1724.
[3] Marquis Du Quesne, Aug. 30th, 1723.

Several have offered, but they know nothing of business except copying and "could not resolve a simple question in arithmetic".[1] Cook-maids cannot be found ; no modest woman will go except in company with a family. Finally he secures Abraham Marys as a clerk on a three years' indenture, £20 salary with all found and £3 extra for bedding and liquors during the voyage to Jamaica.

Newman had a humble protégée, Mary Jackson, whom he had known as a child-aged three in Newfoundland, daughter of the chaplain of the garrison. When she came to England, " Mr. Secretary Addison ",[2] on behalf of the Sons of the Clergy Corporation, at Newman's request bound her to a milliner near Soho, " where she acquired such a character of fidelity and skill in the use of her needle as occasion'd my recommending her to Lady Du Quesne when Mrs. Hawson refused to go abroad with her. . . . I have often repented of this office though I meant it for Lady Du Quesne's service, as well as the good of the poor girl." She was the only English servant, her wages were not paid, and dishonourable accusations had been made against her. But one of the Duchess' gentlewomen " gave me such an account of her virtue patience and fidelity in spite of all abuses as oblig'd me to change my opinion ", formerly unfavourable.[3]

The Marquis flourished at first. " I'm glad to hear also that you live very elegantly and get a vast deal of money ", but Newman very soon suggests that he should send money to pay bills in England. His salary was apparently £800 a year, which was insufficient for a man of his habits. He traded in indigo and left the school bills unpaid. So in 1724 Lady Torrington decided to pay the £10 a quarter, previously given to Newman for Du Quesne's account, direct to the school. In March 1726 we learn that Du Quesne has been acquitted on charges made against his conduct, rather to the surprise of his friends. " I can't help wishing you had never concerned yourself in trade, but liv'd frugally, trusting providence on the produce of your command . . . with less envy from your neighbours than by a trade which some people call by very hard names, such as clandestine smugling, illegal etc. And at the same time you

---

[1] Marquis Du Quesne, Oct. 18th, 1723.
[2] Joseph Addison became Under Secretary of State in 1706.
[3] Lady Torrington, Dec. 30th, 1726. In 1724 Newman had bought clothes for Miss Jackson, her sister being too ill to attend to the matter : 2 pairs of thread stockings 13s., 1 pair of morocco leather laced shoes 8s., 1 calamanco laced 7s., 6 ribbon wires 2s., 4 rolls for headdress 2s. £1 12s. in all, which he charged to the Marquis' account.

may be a great loser, you are represented here as a vast trader, and
one that will soon be in a condition to compound all your South
Sea contracts upon very honourable terms." [1] Lady Torrington
had made many efforts to get him a pension or patent up to £500 a
year. She hoped " to gain an interest in Mr. Walpole who is everything but the King and to speak his favour for you ".[2] But Lord
Townshend, with whom she had interceded, said " that your conduct
had so exposed you to the hatred of the people of Jamaica, that it
was impossible for him to recommend you to the King after so many
flagrant proofs of dishonesty in the trust that had been reposed in
you ".[3] Lady Torrington has " paid three guineas for obtaining
a copy of your defence before the General Assembly at Jamaica,
which, when she had read, she was surprized to find so weak and
insufficient for removing the scandalous imputations laid to your
charge ". She is urging a pension of £500 a year on their joint lives
on condition that Du Quesne will have no more to do with trade.
If she is successful, Newman suggests that £100 is reserved for the
children and that he goes to live in Boston on £400. " You may . . .
live in that town more happily than the Governor himself, if you can
be content with a pretty box and garden such as you are well able to
contrive, with a chariot and a pair of horses to take the air with and to
pass your time in amusing your self with a good book at home, and
such friendly society as that town affords, the most like to London for
the way of living of any place that I know in America " (*Ib.*). At
the date of this letter £300 was owing on Du Quesne's account.
No wonder Newman had asked in January 1725 either to have
remittances or to be relieved of his trust, which was very onerous—
there are frequent references to unsuccessful lotteries and one to a
silk worm project at Chelsea which failed. In the same letter
(1726) Newman assured the Marquis of his unfailing devotion to
the children. " I intreat of you to accept with the most candid
interpretation all the harsh expressions in this letter, which tho'
they are wrote with great regret, the friendship I owe you and your
Lady will not suffer me to conceal." May you " find yourself
through the goodness of providence happy by being once more
undone, and disappointed in all your romantick schemes of making
an immense fortune ".

The rest of the story can be told briefly. Early in 1727 the new

[1] Marquis Du Quesne, June 30th, 1726. The Colonial Office Papers
show that he engaged in the prohibited trade with French and Dutch ships.
[2] Marquis Du Quesne, Oct. 12th, 1724.
[3] Marquis Du Quesne, Nov. 4th, 1726.

Governor of Jamaica, Brigadier Hunter, was willing to continue Du Quesne in his command,[1] but found it impossible, the Marquis being so much hated.[2]   In September Newman says that, if you have traded for two years and four-fifths of your creditors agree, you are entitled to a Statute of Bankruptcy, which costs £70 to £100.   He suggests Du Quesne should come home and live incognito, following his wife, who had already returned, bringing a black boy named Pompey, who Lady Torrington insisted should be disposed of immediately.   By November things had reached a crisis and Newman wrote to Lady Torrington that he would wait on her tomorrow. " If they that forgive 7 times do an available act in the sight of him to whose unbounded goodness we ow everything how highly acceptable must they be who can forgive 70 times 7 times.   I flatter my self that there will be no need of arguments to induce your Ladiship to choose rather on the side of immense forgiveness than of implacable resentment." [3]   On the 13th Du Quesne had arrived.   " Go immediately ", writes Newman, " to your lady at Mr. Batchelor's a mantua maker at the end of Duke's Court in St. Martin's-Lane where I will meet you."

The Marquis was acquitted,[4] and settled down " at Teddington for the convenience of being near the Court [5] where the Marquis goes often, and to be near Lady Torrington for the benefit of the coach ".[6]   A new benefactor appears in 1729, Archdeacon Russell of Cork, who has sent a generous remittance enabling him to set up in the wine trade ; the Marquis is now at Lyons.[7]   By 1731 he is doing well and goes to Hampton Court every week to sell wine, to which he presently adds oil, olives etc.   Newman refuses to buy any more wine, he hasn't drunk the last lot.[8]   " The Marquis is in health but still conflicting with adversities in the verge of Court, tho' he has obtain'd a certificate on the second Statute of Bankruptcy against him." [9]   No improvement attended his second return to business.   " He has some promises from a Great Person at Court, but as the performance has been delay'd some years, I doubt there is little dependence on their being brought to execution." [10]   By the end

---

[1] Lady Torrington, Feb. 8th, 1727.
[2] Marquis Du Quesne, May 11th, 1727.
[3] Lady Du Quesne, Aug. 3rd, 1727.
[4] Mr. Du Quesne, at Geneva, Feb. 18th, 1728.   [5] Kew.
[6] Mr. Du Quesne, July 25th, 1728.
[7] Archdeacon Russell, Nov. 6th, 1729.
[8] Marquis Du Quesne, April 11th, 1734.
[9] Lieut. Wm. Du Quesne, at Jamaica, Dec. 24th, 1735.
[10] Mr. Du Quesne, Sept. 13th, 1736.

of 1736 he seems to have disappeared; he is mentioned once more in the correspondence, Newman having discovered him with difficulty on Lady Day 1738. Though, as we have seen, he was alive in 1740 and " starving ".

A few references to Lady Du Quesne will complete her later history. " I am oblig'd by a letter I receiv'd from Madam Du Quesne to let you know that she desires to be excused waiting on your Ladiship the Coronation Day morning to avoid the charges of lying in the town the night before and after it, I am likewise to thank your Ladiship for your great goodness in permitting my friend and I to see your Ladiship the same morning in your robes but we are necessitated to decline accepting that honour, it being the very same hour that all mankind will be getting places to see your Ladiship in the grand procession, and my friend has happen'd to get leave to see the Dutchess of Bolton in her Grace's robes on Tuesday next." [1] In 1729 she was lodging " in Great Maddox Street, behind Hanover Square new Church ", to be near Lady Torrington.[2] In 1735 we find her with Ann " at the Isle of Wight, where they live on the benevolence of their relations ".[3] Finally Newman wishes to say that she has had " the inconsolable affliction of being remov'd by the Duke of Bolton the new Governor of the Isle of Wight from being any longer housekeeper to Carisbrooke Castle ". Her father, Sir Roger Bradshaigh, has done his best for her. Newman hopes that " the remainder of her life will be made as comfortable as can consist with her infirmities of gout and an advanced age ".[4]

To return to the children, whom we left at Chelsea. Newman was assiduous in his visits, which must have been trying, for in January 1725 a year and a quarter's bills were owing, which, as he explained, compelled him to be " very passive to Mr. Lefevre's exactions ". He planned to send them to " a noble free school at St. Albans ", where the fees were lower,[5] but Lady Du Quesne would not hear of their being moved. " I examine the children almost every time I go to Chelsea and hope you will approve of the little rewards I give to encourage 'em, the weekly allowance of 6d. falling short of what is

[1] Lady Torrington, Oct. 7th, 1727. The Duchess is the first wife, not the famous Lavinia Fenton (Polly Peachum), whom the Duke married in 1752.   [2] Archdeacon Russell, Nov. 6th, 1729.
[3] But both ladies were able to get Newman to buy lottery tickets for them in the State lottery for building Westminster Bridge.
[4] Sir Thomas Lowther, of Holker, Aug. 17th, 1742. The Duke was Governor of the Island from 1726 to 1733 and again from 1742 to 1746.
[5] Marquis Du Quesne, Nov. 17th, 1724.

necessary to keep them in heart with the other children." [1]   He had
them to stay with him and arranged visits to friends, such as the
Ducanes.[2] They were too young, he decided, for dancing lessons,
but Mrs. Lefevre was strictly charged to " make them sit and walk
straight ".

Harry was evidently the favourite and his return to England
was greeted with enthusiasm. " Last night little Harry lay at my
chambers [in the Middle Temple] in good health ", Newman wrote
to Lady Torrington on Oct. 15th, 1724, though the child was
suffering from skin trouble caused by the long voyage and salt
provisions. " The voyage being very long, they were oblig'd to
kill their catts and dogs to help out their provision, not that they eat
'em themselves but to save water and to feed the tiger and other wild
creatures which my Lord Duke has sent over to the King." For the
present Lady Manningham, wife of the doctor, will take him into
her nursery. Where is he to go after that ? Chelsea is too expensive.
The two boys cost £72 1s. 4d. last year, clothes and linen extra, but
including fourteen pairs of shoes bought for them. Any nursery
near London will take Harry for £13 a year, £16 when he reaches
the stage of learning Latin.

The little boy was a handful. " Harry grows as wild as a
buck, and his spirit enough for six children." [3] The problem was
temporarily solved by sending him to board with Mrs. Hawson,
Lady Du Quesne's former maid, and to a " Dame School " in the
neighbourhood of Chelsea College.[4] But in a few weeks' time
Harry had gone to a boys' school, being " too ungovernable for a
mistress . . . the master pins him to his gown ". A year later
Newman wrote to the Marquis : " I put him into breeches on the
King's birthday, which he likes so well that, with his good will, he
would go to bed with them, and never put them off."

[1] Marquis Du Quesne, Aug. 14th, 1723.
[2] Mr. Ducane was a Director of the Bank of England. "He is vastly
rich and values himself much upon being related to your family " (Mr.
Montross Du Quesne, Feb. 13th, 1724). In 1728 he added £20 to the sums
being disbursed by Lady Torrington for the Marquis. His ancestor came
to England in 1570 escaping from the Alva Massacres.
[3] Mr. Du Quesne, March 11th, 1725.
[4] Lady Du Quesne, June 25th, 1725. In the same letter Newman says
that Lady Torrington and Sir Richard Manningham refuse to let him be
inoculated against smallpox without his mother's leave. As elsewhere he
says that Billy and Tommy have had smallpox and got over it quickly, but
unfortunately Harry has escaped, the term " smallpox " may have been
used to cover chickenpox.

In January 1727 the two elder boys were sent to St. Albans Abbey School. Newman wrote a letter to the master, the Rev. Mr. Fothergill, to go with them. The bearer (Mrs. Daws) will pay the entrance fee of a guinea each. They have brought with them the books used in the French school. Both have had the smallpox and speak and read French and English. Allow them 6d. a week pocket money, not to be spent on fruit or nuts. Harry will be coming six months hence, when he will be $5\frac{3}{4}$ years, but he is "a rugged child". Billy has learned to dance, but Newman has no instructions about continuing lessons. He will be eleven years old tomorrow. "I shall be always glad to hear of their welfare, and desire they would write to me in French till they can do it in Latin." [1]

In March Lady Torrington was trying to get H.R.H. the Princess to take Billy as a page when he was old enough. The sequel appears in a letter written by Newman on December 5th, 1727, which deserves to be quoted almost in full.

> Dear Billy,
> I thank you for your letter of the 26th of last month which I received at Madam Du Quesne's when the postman brought hers, and I am glad to find you mend in your writing, as I hope you do in your knowledge of the Latin and French tongues. . . . I hope also that you are design'd for a great comfort and blessing to your parents and brothers in whatever station of life the providence of God may call you to though there is as your mother desires me to tell you no likelihood at present of your being admitted to the honour of waiting on Her Majesty as one of her pages, from some hints that have been lately given to your Mamma, but don't let this discourage you, it may be you want to be humbled, and have in conversation boasted too much of the honour your friends aim'd at for you. . . . Believe me to be
>
> dear Billy
> Your most humble servant.

Newman had other plans for Billy. He had consulted two Custom-house officers, who agreed that it should be possible to get a Patent Place in London or on the coast for William, which would "be a comfortable support to him and all the family, and whenever he comes to be prefer'd to Her Majesty's service, it may be resign'd to one of his brothers. These places are all capable of being officiated by a deputy, the salaries of them paid quarterly out of the customhouse." [2] Nothing came of this and in 1732 Billy "by my Lady Torrington's interest with Sir Robert Walpole is a young clerk in the lottery office, which he attends every day from his father's house" in Old

---

[1] Jan. 10th, 1727, which gives us the date of Billy's birth.
[2] Lady Torrington, Oct. 7th, 1727.

Bond Street. Then in 1734 he joined the Army, as a lieutenant in one of the Independent Companies.[1] Newman had misgivings about his going to Jamaica, but said my Lord Torrington [2] could get leave for him to return for a commission in three years' time.

Newman wrote a long letter to " Dear Master Du Quesne " on Dec. 24th, 1735, giving all the news of the family. He proceeded : " Dear Billy, though heaven witholds from you some of the blessings which others lavishly enjoy, I hope you will live to see the clouds dispersed ". He urges him to study nature and the management of a plantation, with a view to the future. " When you are quartered in a desolate place let the Holy Scripture or some other good book be your daily amusement and if you can inspire the soldiers under your command with a love of virtue and religion when they are destitute of every advantage for acquiring it, such heroism will make you the darling of God and men and add a glorious lustre to your account hereafter. Adieu my dear Billy . . ." The poor boy died of a fever after a year or two.

There is nothing similar about Thomas, except that Col. Townsend, who had married Lady Torrington's niece, undertook the whole cost of his education,[3] and that he was " design'd for the University of Cambridge " in the summer of 1738.

Poor William ! good sober Thomas ! and poor Harry too ! How long he remained at St. Albans is not told but in the summer of 1736 (aged fourteen) he returned home from the West Indies in a man-of-war and quartered himself on Newman. " To prevent his hindering my clerk and molesting the tranquility of my little family, I have been oblig'd to put him to a writing school in my neighbour-hood, but when I sent yesterday to know whether he was there, he was not, nor had been there all the forenoon, being gone to Tyburn to see the men hang'd, a curiosity I can't blame him for." [4] He was then sent to a better school at Chelsea, from which he was expelled, when Newman arranged for him to go to Mr. Stothard's Academy. In the spring of 1737 he went to sea again. " Coming home last Saturday evening I was surpriz'd with the sight of Harry Du Quesne who gave me no reasonable account of his leaving the Gloucester but that he had nothing to do." [5] He had worked

---

[1] Mr. Montross Du Quesne, Sept. 13th, 1736.
[2] The second Viscount (Byng), no relation to the Lady T. of these letters. " Commission " in the regular Army (?).
[3] Marquis Du Quesne, Aug. 12th, 1736.
[4] Marquis Du Quesne, Aug. 12th, 1736.
[5] Sir Roger Bradshaigh, Dec. 26th, 1737.

his passage home from Gibraltar to Amsterdam in a Dutch ship and then to Harwich, " from whence he footed it up to London ". He was at once induced to volunteer for the *Hampton Court*, bound for Jamaica.   Newman wrote him an encouraging letter to Spithead, gently reproaching him for the sleepless nights he had given his mother and sister.   Harry was promised the first vacancy as a midshipman and, though only a ship's boy, was invited to dine with the officers, but on reaching Jamaica he deserted.   A final letter, after which he disappears, recommends him to Captain Douglas of the *Falmouth* as one who has had experience of the West Indies, Gibraltar, Cadiz and Holland.

I have left the fortunes of Ann to the last, in order to end on a cheerful note.   As early as 1724 Newman begins to weave a possible romance.   Describing Mr. Ducane's call, with his two sons, aged twelve and thirteen, who are at St. Paul's School, he says that perhaps one of them will come and fetch " Mrs. Ann " home one day.[1] " Miss at Geneva is well.   I sent her 3 pairs of shoes t'other day." [2] He has received a letter from Miss Du Quesne " with an apology for her not writing to me in English ".[3]   Lady Torrington sent £10 10s. for her education in 1727, not to be used on dancing or music lessons.   Mr. Du Quesne [4] wrote in 1728 saying that she goes to a half boarding school at 8 a.m., returning at 6 p.m. ;   she learns religion, good manners, and several works fit for a gentlewoman.   The Marquise can do no more.   " My brother has ruined her to such a degree that she has no more than fifty pounds a year left."   He pleads for help from Lady Torrington, who " has no children and is very rich, my mother has her own children to entertain and can scarce do it ".   In May, Ann came to England.   Newman wrote that she is " just now come from Geneva, wonderfully improv'd for her age as to be in danger of being, through her beauty and accomplishments, the toast of the town ".

A letter to Geneva [5] giving news of " Miss " provides a pretty domestic picture and suggests that the days of the strong silent Englishmen were yet to come.

She is now at board at Twickenham under my Lady Torrington's protection, where she learns English apace ; I have not seen her since

[1] Mr. Du Quesne, Feb. 13th, 1724.
[2] Lady Du Quesne, July 9th, 1724.
[3] Lady Du Quesne, June 25th, 1725.   So the English letter quoted above was dictated to her.
[4] Some of whose letters are copied into the book.
[5] Mr. Du Quesne, July 25th, 1728.

she went, but my Lady Torrington and the Marquis both tell me that she improves very much, so that Lady Du Quesne, her mother, can now freely converse with her, which she could not do for a long time, but by signs which gave her some uneasiness.

I told my Lady Torrington that she had learnt 105 Psalms by heart at Geneva, but I was afraid she would forget 'em at an English school, upon which her Ladyship assur'd me she would take upon her to make her repeat 'em as often as she came to see her. Miss has a tender remembrance of her grandmother's kindness to her, and I could never mention her with that respect as I ought, but Miss put her handkerchief to her eyes ;—a remarkable instance of which happen'd once when I had receiv'd a letter from your good mother to the Marquis, which I immediately carried to him, but he not being at home, his lady open'd it and desir'd me to read it for fear it might require a speedy answer, not knowing that it was from Geneva. When it was open'd, and found to be from Lady Du Quesne, Miss with great impatience desired to know what her grandmother said of her, and when I came to that part of the letter where her Ladyship had spoke of her with great affection, she burst into a torrent of tears, and I could not help bearing her company, so that I had not power to go on reading the letter.

Madame Du Quesne finding us both crying, was afraid there was bad news in the letter, and with great concern desired me to explain it, which when I had done, she laugh'd to see us cry for an occasion of joy. . . .

When Ann grew up Newman and her mother tried to arrange a marriage. " I took an opportunity to acquaint Mr. B. with the contents of it [your letter], but he told me frankly that tho' he had a great respect for the young lady you mention'd, he is under those strict obligations to govern himself by his father's directions in an affair of that moment that he dare not indulge himself in any inclinations to alter his condition without his consent, that being a younger brother and newly entering into the business of a laborious profession which has been very expensive hitherto. . . ." [1] (This is evidently Jonathan Belcher, of the Middle Temple, second son of the Governor of New England.) Ann had ideas of her own. Miss Du Quesne " din'd with me last Sunday senight, when she assur'd me she had laid aside all thoughts of marriage to a Scotch jeweller who had made his addresses to her ".[2]

Just before Newman's death in 1743 he was able to see the girl married whom he had loved (as a second father) since childhood. He wrote to Jonathan Belcher on March 31st :

Miss Du Quesne whom you had bespoke as a second, was happily marry'd the 17th current to Mr. John French only son of a gentleman

[1] Lady Du Quesne, May 13th, 1738.
[2] Mrs. Chamberlayne, Dec. 14th, 1738.

of the Isle of Wight, a discreet man in good circumstances, who was so pleas'd with Miss's charms that he told his parents he could think of no other person, and that he should think himself happy to have her tho' without any fortune. Sir Roger and Lady Bradshaigh [grand-parents] with her principal friends readily agreed to the proposal and Sir Roger offer'd them a wedding dinner, but he politely excus'd accepting it, because he had some friends from the Isle of Wight who had complemented him with their company on the occasion that could not be so free at Sir Roger's table as at his.

IV

SOME NOTES ON CHARITY SCHOOLS

For a full account of the Charity Schools the reader is referred to Miss M. G. Jones' *The Charity School Movement*. All I propose to do here is to contribute some notes to her book derived from the S.P.C.K. archives and publications.

(a) ANNIVERSARY SERMONS

A volume is preserved containing the Anniversary Sermons arranged by the S.P.C.K. and preached in connection with the Charity Schools from 1704 to 1728, all of them on Thursday in Whitsun Week.[1] The first service was held at St. Andrew's, Holborn, the subsequent ones at St. Sepulchre's, until 1737, when the service was transferred to St. Paul's Cathedral.[2] The sermons illustrate the ideas in the minds of the promoters of the movement.

Dean Willis, of Lichfield, was the first preacher. The schools are for the children of the poor. Our purpose is " to repair the breaches made by the wickedness of the present age " in all classes. It may be assumed that only those who try to bring up their own children well will be ready to subscribe. He tells his more fortunate hearers that the family is a society, which owes worship to God. You must control your children, subdue their passions, and teach religion. " But I do not mean by all this, to encourage a sheepish temper in children, tho' I think that is better than the contrary extreme." You must not be too ambitious for your children. Turning to the Charity Schools, he says there are 50 in London ; many of the children are clothed, some are maintained wholly, and the number of schools increases all the time. Their objects are to teach Christianity, to qualify the children for honest employment, and to put them out to some trade.

In 1705 Dean Stanhope, of Canterbury, maintains that " the poor have always a right to some part of the possessions of the rich " and refers to " the yearly processions of the little eleemosinaries " to the service.

White Kennet, Archdeacon of Huntingdon, afterwards Bishop

[1] Cp. W. Blake : " 'Twas on a Holy Thursday, their innocent faces clean, The children walking two and two, in red and blue and green."
[2] The 1877 service was the last.

of Peterborough, was the preacher in 1706. He says that the children
who come to the service " walk in decent couples thro' the streets,
led by the ministers ". They often transform their homes by their
examples. " The greatest disorders in any neighbourhood do most
commonly proceed from the folly of children." Without the
schools " the poor ragged children would swarm like locusts in our
streets and by playing about, with lies, and oaths, and filthy language
in their mouths, they would corrupt the children of the better sort ".
He emphasizes that they, unlike the Grammar Schools, provide
for girls. There are 1500 boys and 1000 girls in the London Charity
Schools. £3000 a year is raised by subscriptions, in addition to
special gifts and collections, most of the children receive clothing,
and many of the schools have been endowed.

Dr. Smalridge, Dean of Christ Church, in 1710 paid a tribute to
" the Royal Benefactress ", Queen Anne, and drew a comparison
between her and Pharaoh's daughter. Dr. Moss in 1708 spoke of
the decay of virtue in " this degenerate people " of England, and
Bishop Dawes, of Chester, in 1713 referred to the many who were
unemployed and starving ; " whippings, pilloryings, and executions
are common ". The Rev. Lord Willoughby de Broke in 1712
drew a pleasing picture of the piety of Church people. " Never
were our churches so well filled ; never our Communions so
frequented ; never more holy zeal, more humble devotion ; never
larger charities, than what are constantly offered up at the Holy
Table in every church of this great city "—the improvement is due
largely to the Queen. Subsequent preachers included three eminent
Bishops—Edmund Gibson, Thomas Sherlock, and Thomas Wilson.
Bishop Talbot, of Salisbury, in 1717 drew attention to the results of
neglecting girls' education, seen in " that lewd tribe of night-
walkers " from " hellish brothel houses ". And in 1723 Dr. Waterland told of a plan (which came to nothing) to erect " a Superior
School, for the training up of school-masters and school-mistresses ".

(b) Finance

The Society helped the Charity Schools by propaganda, directly
and through its correspondents urging their establishment ; by
advice, and in particular by drawing up model rules ; by helping
in cases of need, starting new schools and paying off debts ; and
by transmitting earmarked gifts. Its income was always small and
there was no attempt to raise a central fund. Indeed in those days

the principle of local self-help was strongly implanted in the minds of Englishmen. So the references to money matters in the minutes consist mainly of reports showing what had been done by local effort. The following extracts from unpublished minutes dealing with the schools, covering the period from December 1704 to March 1707, will illustrate what was going on.

1704.

December 17th. A collection for the Charity Schools at the doors of Aldersgate Church last Sunday amounted to £13 5s. At Hampton Lovett 17 children are kept at school out of the offertory money.

1705.

January 18th. £80 has been collected at St. Margaret's, Westminster, £85 at St. Anne's, Soho.

February 1st. St. Martin-in-the-Fields has a plan for a school for 80 boys and 50 girls. £30 a year is promised from the offertory money, £40 a year from lottery tickets for six years to come, and an Army debenture of £80 has been bought.

May 4th. The Archbishop has subscribed largely to a Charity School at York. So have the Dean and Chapter, the Lord Mayor and Aldermen, and others. £100 a year is secured for the present. The boys are clothed and fed, and do some manual work. The ladies of the city are raising £60 a year for a girls' school.

June 14th. £8 a year has been bequeathed by a gentlewoman to the school at Aldgate. " 'Twas observ'd that all the poor children walked very solemnly before her corps and each person invited had one of Dr. Kennet's Christian Scholars given to him instead of a pair of gloves." At Northill, in Bedfordshire, the minister pays for all the children; at Southill, 12 are taught at the minister's expense.

September 13th. £24 a year is paid to the master at Tunbridge Wells plus £2 for firing. It is intended to clothe all the boys.

October 25th. Here we have an unexpected reference to the young men of the Religious Societies, who teach many of the children and bring them to church.

December 13th. The Corporation of Leeds have given a fair house for the boys' school.

1706.

March 14th. Several Oxfordshire villages have a monthly Communion Service, the offerings at which are devoted to Charity

Schools. The Archbishop of Canterbury's lady has begun a school at Lambeth, with 12 girls, whom she is to clothe.

May 2nd. At Winlaton in Co. Durham the men of the iron-foundry, 400 to 500 in number, have agreed to the deduction of ¼d. out of every 1/- of their wages for the relief of their own poor and the education of their children.

September 12th. Three schools have been opened at Bury St. Edmunds. The mistresses are paid £12 10s. each per annum. The boys are provided with two caps and two neckcloths apiece, the girls with two coifs.

September 26th. Specimens of the clothes of the London Charity children have been sent to Norwich.

November 21st. Mr. Chamberlayne has settled £10 per annum on the school at Chelsea, £5 to educate five poor children, £5 towards putting them out as apprentices.

1707.

January 9th. The Bishop has given £40 a year to the school at Salisbury, which enables 30 boys and 20 girls to be taught to read, write, and cast accounts; also to be clothed. Children who spin earn up to 2/6d. a week, or more. A few other children are supported by other benefactors.

February 13th. The Charity School at Warwick is well managed by the Corporation without the help or advice of the clergy. Yarmouth reports that boys as young as 8 are encouraged to go to sea, while the war lasts.

February 27th. Mr. Lightmaker of Horsted Keynes has built a house and settled it on the school, with £20 a year tax free. The schoolmaster is to teach 20 boys for this and is allowed to take 20 more in order to earn extra remuneration.

March 6th. The cost at Maldon, Essex, is £1 a year per boy, plus £2 for his clothes. Newbury, Berks., has 20 boys, towards whose education the Corporation pays £40 a year. Subscriptions are also received, and books are bought out of the offertory money in church.

March 27th. At Haverfordwest, in Wales, 25 children are taught and clothed, parents receiving a maintenance grant of £1 a child per year.

There are many references in the minutes to endowed schools on similar lines before the establishment of Charity Schools, and many legacies to particular schools are reported.

(c) A TEACHER'S MANUAL

The Christian School-Master: *or, The Duty of those who are Employ'd in the Publick Instruction of Children*: *Especially in Charity-Schools*, by James Talbott, D.D. (1707), was dedicated " To the Right Reverend and Right Honourable the Lords, and all the rest of the Members of the Society for Promoting Christian Knowledge ". The Society had formally commissioned the book and paid for its production. It was used as a Manual for Teachers throughout the eighteenth century and must have had a great influence.[1]

The teacher's three qualifications are patriotism, virtue, learning— in this order. (A country which looked back to the Civil War in the recent past and was looking forward with anxiety to a disputed succession when Queen Anne died, anxiety which was justified by the Jacobite risings of 1715 and 1745, could not afford the luxury of uncontrolled education.) Schoolmasters had to be loyal members of the Church of England, " which is certainly an essential part of the English Constitution ", and to abjure the Pretender. It was " highly reasonable, that those who have such frequent opportunities of instilling what principles they think fit into the minds of young people, should give all possible security to the publick, that they do not entertain any which are contrary to, or inconsistent with the present Establishment in Church and State ".

Religion, and good morals which are its fruit, are the second qualification, for without a good example teaching is fruitless. The virtues especially necessary in the master are patience and humility, sagacity, equity, forbearance, sweetness of disposition, diligence, piety. Negatively, he must not accept gifts from parents " on any pretence whatsoever; these schools being only designed for the education of such poor children, whose parents or friends are not able to give them learning ". The idea is that ability to give presents proves ability to pay fees; also the master is tempted to be partial.

Learning refers to such things as the master is required to teach; education for the Universities or for the " more eminent professions " is excluded from the scope of the book. The newly appointed teacher must learn from visiting other schools and giving lessons in them under supervision. He should not be under 25, and must be free from deformity of person or defect of speech. He is under the minister of the parish, who will vouch at least for his religious qualifications with a view to his being licensed by the Ordinary.

[1] It is briefly treated in Miss Jones' book.

F

As soon as possible the children must learn the Catechism, which is taught exhaustively on two days of the week (Saturday being one), and home prayers. The Duty towards God and my Neighbour is taught constantly. Special care must be taken to eradicate swearing, envy of fellow pupils, lying (the besetting sin of children), and tale-bearing—children must conceal and excuse one another's faults, unless " commanded by their superiors to speak what they know, for the discovery of something that may be more amiss than they are aware of ". Justice in bargaining is inculcated; faults must not be pretended in what is bought or concealed in what is sold, " in those petty bargains they make with one another ". Fighting, encouraged by parents who like to see " hopeful signs of mettle and spirit ", must be put down, as also cruelty to the weaker children and to animals. One third of the whole book of 144 pages is devoted to these ethical matters.

Reading is the main subject taught, especially of the Bible and Prayer Book, and for the senior scholars *The Whole Duty of Man*; but pleasant and profitable books should sweeten the children's labours. Arithmetic is taught sufficiently to make them expert in the ordinary keeping of accounts.

There are four classes : the first learns the rudiments of reading, in the horn-book, primer and spelling-book; the second reads the Psalter and New Testament; the third reads the whole Bible and learns to write; the fourth, having learned to write well, is taught arithmetic.

One difficulty is the absence of Latin from the curriculum. The meanest husbandman is unwilling to take his child away from school until a smattering of Latin has been learned. The little that could be taught would soon be forgotten and prove useless, nor would it be any help in English composition to be able to construe a few Latin words and to repeat the admired *Propria quae maribus*.

School hours are 7 to 11 and 1 to 5 in the summer half year, 8 to 11 and 1 to 4 in the winter. The roll-call is read and prayers are said. All children must be sent to school washed and combed. Home work is set on Saturdays. Holidays are three weeks at Christmas and one week at Easter and at Whitsuntide. Absence at harvest time to help in gleaning is not allowed, because of the danger of bad company. When manual work is combined with book learning, a good plan is for each boy to have one hour of the latter at both morning and afternoon school. When dinner is provided great care must be taken over manners; after the meal a story from the Bible is read by an elder boy on Sundays and Holy-days, at other times a fable from Aesop. Recreation is left to the children's own devices, provided they do not trangress the limits of ground assigned.

In endowed foundations, that is boarding schools, prayers are said night and morning, besides the children's short private prayers. The former may be taken by the elder boys. The children go to church twice on Sundays, and on all Holy-days; they bow on entering the church and kneel down to pray privately. None may join in the singing who has not learned the tunes perfectly. The children must behave reverently, sitting in some conspicuous part of the church and bowing at the Holy Name. They are periodically catechized by the minister and should be asked questions about the sermon on their return from church.

Discipline is preserved by rewards and punishments. Rewards take the form of praise and promotion, punishments that of reproof, degradation in class, corporal correction, and, as a last resort and only for the sake of the others, expulsion. The rod must be used with great discretion and the child must be shown the justice of the punishment. Chastisement should be inflicted with sedateness, interposing admonishments between the blows.

Finally, the Visiting Committee, representing the benefactors, play an important part. The children must be taught to realize that they owe their education to them, and to God who has inspired them.

The pastoral nature of the schoolmaster's office is shown in the prayer provided for his private use, which contains these petitions :—

" Possess my mind with a just and tender regard for those precious souls committed to my charge ; that I may watch over them, as one that must give an account, that I may do it with joy and not with grief. And forasmuch as the form of knowledge and of godliness, without the power, will neither be profitable to me, nor to those that hear me ; grant me thy grace, that I may take heed to my self as to my instructions ; that while I teach others, I my self may not be a cast-away ; but may shew myself in all things a pattern of good works, an example to these young believers, in word, in conversation, in charity, in spirit, in faith, in purity ; that my profiting may appear unto all for their edification.

" Neither pray I for my self alone, but for the children which thou hast given me : that they may be followers of me, as I am of Christ.

Sanctifie them with thy truth, and preserve them in it; that not one of this little flock may be lost in the day of the Lord Jesus. . . ."

Another example of the spiritual side of the teaching is seen in Bishop White Kennet's *The Christian Scholar: in Rules and Directions for Children and Youth, sent to English Schools. Especially design'd for the Poor Boys Taught and Cloathed by Charity.* Among other blessings, the boys are to thank God's mercy that they are not cripples or changelings. On entering church "pay some due reverence by putting off thy hat, bowing thy head, bending thy knee, and the like". Make a resolve: "I will at first sight of my parents in the morning, and in my last taking leave at nightfall on my knees before them, and say to this effect: Pray Father (or Mother) bless me, and beg God's blessing on me, to make me his faithful servant and your obedient child." The following advice could not be bettered: "Make no needless complaints against [other children]. Tell no silly stories of them. Indeed when your Governors command, you must tell the truth. But otherwise, conceal their faults, and excuse their little follies, to save them from anger, and to deliver them from punishment." "Reverence the Bishops" he says elsewhere "as spiritual fathers; bow down and kneel before them; ask their blessing, because good old custom so obtained." To London boys especially he gives the following charge: "I presume thou art charged strictly by thy master, to meet no minister in the streets, without putting off thy cap, and bowing down the head. A method of piety and good manners, that will much help to reclaim this city, and in time to reform this nation."

(d) A READER

The Reader most used was Francis Fox's *Introduction to Spelling and Reading*, compiled originally for the Charity School of St. Mary's, Reading, and reprinted in a revised form as late as 1818. It vividly recreates the atmosphere of a school. The alphabet is interesting in that the names of two letters are pronounced differently from what we are accustomed to: j is sometimes "jod", z is "ze". The list of monosyllabic nouns signifying apparel runs thus: "cloth stuff pluck silk lawn coat cloak frock hood shirt shift smock gown band cap hat coif hose sock shoes boots pumps gloves chain ring scarf". The following list is given of "Play, and terms used in them": "game cards chess draughts die dice race dance cross and pile pell-mell leap jump ball bowls win lose trumps lurch stake ace duce tray quoit whipe scourge top gig sport ".

At lesson XXIV the first consecutive readings begin. They are based on the Bible, starting with Genesis. This series ends with the death of Samson in lesson XLII; XLIII–XLIX teach dogma; L–LVI are Scripture texts bearing on behaviour; LVII–LXVI are proverbs and sayings of famous men. Part II gives detailed instructions about abbreviations, punctuation, the division of syllables etc.

(e) A LETTER TO PRINCESS SOPHIA

After 1715 the Charity Schools had a sad set-back, for they were suspected of being seedplots of Jacobitism. That the S.P.C.K. had no sympathy with it is proved by a letter dated August 3rd, 1713, written by Henry Newman, its Secretary, on behalf of the Society to Princess Sophia, mother of George I.

To the Princess Sophia.

May it please your Highness

Every loyal Englishman is ambitious to lay at your feet some acknowledgment of the duty and affection he ows to your illustrious person and family. And tho' the tribute accompanying this be so small yet as it is the offering of an honest heart, it may perhaps be as acceptable as if it had been greater. Your Highness will with pleasure observe therein the care that is taken to preserve the Protestant Religion in these Kingdoms by providing a means of instruction for the poor who at present make too considerable a part of the nation to be neglected. And tho' the method of Charity Schools has been of but about 15 or 16 years standing it has pleas'd God so wonderfully to prosper the design that above 1000 schools have been erected in that time at which above 20 thousand poor children are now instructed and about 10 thousand more have been put out apprentices.

This has laid such a foundation for securing the Protestant Religion and of consequence the succession of your illustrious family to the throne of these Kingdoms as will I hope for ever frustrate all attempts to introduce Popery or overthrow the settlement on which the future happiness of this nation so much depends.

Your Highness may be pleas'd to know that the chief promoters of this good work are a voluntary Society consisting of about 500 gentlemen living in almost all parts of the Kingdom, who by their purses and good offices contribute all they can to promote Christian Knowledge.

Madam,

In confidence that an account of these little nurseries that are so well design'd would not be unacceptable it is humbly laid at your Highness's feet as a testimony of the profound sense of duty in,

Madam,

Your Royal Highness's most obedient and
most humbly devoted servant.

(f) Workhouse Schools

(1) A very full description is found in *An Account of Several Workhouses for employing and maintaining the Poor . . . as also of several Charity Schools for Promoting Work and Labour* (2nd edition, 1732). The schools in connection with the workhouses were in many cases a charitable work. Wellwishers were invited to undertake the cost of one or more children. The boys and girls, like the aged and infirm poor, had to work with their hands. The discipline was strict, but, judged by contemporary standards, not unduly so. The following details may be of interest.

At Bishopsgate there were two divisions, the Steward's side for the respectable poor and the Keeper's side for vagabonds, etc. There was a chapel. The children, who numbered 129, had two hours a day schooling. As a specimen of the food provided we quote the menu for Wednesday : " Breakfast, bread and butter or cheese. Dinner, plumb dumplings. Supper, bread and butter or cheese." " In summer time, pease, beans, greens, and roots are allowed, as the season affords them."

St. Andrew's, Holborn, Workhouse is described with minute detail, the household accounts being printed in full. Beef cost $2\frac{1}{2}d.$ a lb., cheese $3\frac{1}{4}d.$ In a week sixty-two persons consumed 116 lb. of meat and 89 gallons of beer. The inmates rose at 5 in summer, 6 in winter, and went to bed at 8 in winter, 9 in summer. Every room was washed out three times a week in summer. The worst punishment, for a persistent liar, was to be set on a stool at dinner-time with " a paper fixed on his or her breast, with these words wrote, *Infamous Liar* ". All this seems to refer to children as well as to adults, but oakum-picking, which is here optimistically viewed, was not, one hopes, a child's occupation—" they that pick ockam are continually refresh'd with the balsamick odour of it ".

The Girls' School at Greenwich is held up as a model. It was entirely managed by charitable ladies, who devised punishments based on shame rather than fear. Each girl had a peg which was put in the highest of seven vertical holes. At each offence the peg was moved downward. When it reached the fifth hole, the girl was looked on as " a high criminal ". If this treatment did not melt the heart, a rod was pinned on to the child. The girls made all their own clothes, and were taught to read, write, " cast accompts ", and say the Catechism ; they attended church daily.

The Quaker Workhouse at Clerkenwell receives great praise.

A daily cold bath was available for any who wished it. This was far in advance of the age. A manual of deportment called *The Young Man's Own Book*, published about 1800, refers with approval to the custom which was recently begun, in England only, of washing certain parts of the body daily.

At Wisbech the boys and girls slept three, the elderly people two, in a bed. The food was liberal : " good beef, dumplins, pease-porridge, milk-porridge, bread and cheese ; the quantity according to every one's stomach at noon "—less at the other meals.

The children at Ware spent half the day at their books and earned but little. At Beverley workers were given an incentive in the shape of 2*d*. in the 1*s*. on all their earnings.

At the end of the book the Rules for Charity Schools are printed, signed by all the Bishops. A note follows to the effect that the Rules have been laid before the S.P.C.K., which has adopted and printed them, sending them to all Charity Schools in South-Britain. In so far as the activities described in the volume were the duties laid by law on the parish authorities the Bishops and the S.P.C.K. would not be concerned. But the schools attached to the workhouses were clearly under ecclesiastical supervision.

(g) Welsh Circulating Schools

Thomas Gouge, a minister expelled on St. Bartholomew's Day, 1662, went to Wales and started schools which, according to Strype, were the origin of the S.P.C.K. Charity Schools. The later movement here to be described was due to the Rev. Griffith Jones, " Minister of Llandowror" in Carmarthenshire, a forgotten hero who must have been one of the noblest priests of the post-Reformation Church. It is described in an affecting book called *Welch Piety : or a Collection of the several Accounts of the Welch Circulating Charity Schools, from their first Rise in the year 1737, to Michaelmas 1752.* Funds were raised mainly in London, one of the Treasurers being " Mr Francis Gosling, Banker in Fleet Street "—ancestor of the present General Secretary of S.P.C.K. The 1738 Report describes the origin of the movement. Mr. Jones began by catechizing " after the Second Lesson in Divine Service upon Saturdays before Sacrament Sundays "—adults as well as children. Out of this grew a school, erected out of "the Sacrament money". Already thirty-seven schools were in existence and 2400 pupils were enrolled. The schools were " circulating " ; that is, they remained for three or four months in one place, and returned the following year for an equal period. The pupils learned the Catechism, Scripture texts, and the Faith generally, besides being taught to read the Bible. The schools were held in the months September to May, and lasted four or five hours a day. When farmers would not release their labourers, the Charity helped them to pay substitutes; or they stayed away and were fed by charity. The books were provided by S.P.C.K., which in the first year sent 740 Bibles, many Psalters and Catechisms, and 13,000 other books—all in Welsh. Often the church building was used. The 1739 Report deals with the objection " that the Irish is abolishing, by means of the English Charity-Schools in the Highlands of Scotland, and beginning to be so by the same institutions in Ireland, and that the Bishop of Man has found means to bring the Manks into disuse "—then why perpetuate Welsh ? The reply is that the people can only be taught in Welsh, and that Welsh literature is the chastest in Europe; when taught to read a person cannot find atheism or immorality in the language. A little later we learn that Sunday dancing is being given up, but " the old way is still kept up, of dressing in the bear's skin in order to baiting ". The monthly Eucharist is now thronged with devout worshippers. At Puncheston, Pembrokeshire, the church can hardly hold them. Eglwys Helen, in Glamorganshire, reports that the monthly communicants number 120, whereas before there was a sparsely attended celebration three times a year. In the first years two-thirds of the scholars were adults. The last Report is dated 1760—there may be later ones elsewhere. The high-water mark was reached in 1757, when 218 schools were at work with 9834 scholars. These figures are exclusive of night schools, which presumably continued the work. These Welsh parish priests sowed the seed faithfully, but the harvest was reaped in the main by the Methodists.

V

THE HOMILIES

THE Book of Common Prayer sets the doctrinal standards of Anglicanism, containing as it does the rites used continually by priests and people alike.   By its side are the Thirty-nine Articles of Religion to which the clergy have to " assent " at ordination and on other occasions (the present modified formula dates from 1865).   A third set of formularies is provided by the Homilies, which are prescribed by the Prayer Book as an alternative to the Sermon, and characterized in the Articles as containing " godly and wholesome doctrine ".

Many of the clergy would confess to ignorance if challenged about the Homilies ; the very name provokes an indulgent smile.   But the prominent place they hold in our formularies makes it desirable that we should know a little about this first " omnibus " volume of sermons in the English language.

The first part was published in 1547, Cranmer and others being the authors.   The second part, to which Jewel was the main contributor, was finished in 1563, except for the last homily, inspired by the rebellion of the Earls of Northumberland and Westmorland in 1569, but was not authorized till 1571.   There are thirty-three in all, varying in length considerably.   Some are quite short, for they are generally divided into two or more parts, and it is suggested that they be read one half in the forenoon, the other in the afternoon. In some cases a portion of a Homily ends with the ascription, which shows that a complete discourse is intended.   The first section of the Homily on Almsdeeds contains about 2400 words, and need not have taken more than twenty-five minutes to deliver with deliberate diction.   The style for the most part is admirable.   The following passage is typical of many.

Neither grudged she [the blessed Virgin Mary] at the length and tediousness of the journey from Nazareth to Bethlehem, from whence and whither she must go to be taxed, neither repined she at the sharpness of the dead time of winter, being the latter end of December, an unhandsome time to travel in, specially a long journey, for a woman being in her case ; but, all excuses set apart, she obeyed and came to the appointed place : where at her coming she found such great resort and throng of people, that, finding no place in any inn, she was fain, after her long, painful, and tedious journey, to take up her lodging in a stable, where also she was delivered of her blessed Child ; and this also declareth how near her time she took that journey. This obedience of this most noble and most virtuous lady to a foreign and pagan prince doth well teach us, who in comparison to her are most base and vile, what ready obedience we do owe to our natural and gracious sovereign (*Against Wilful Rebellion.*)

Or again:

Consider the decay of the towns nigh the seas, which should be most ready by the number of the people there to repulse the enemy; and we which dwell further off upon the land, having them as our buckler to defend us, should be the more in surety. If they be our neighbours, why should we not wish them to prosper? If they be our defence, as nighest at hand to repel the enemy, to keep out the rage of the seas, which else would break upon our fair pastures, why should we not cherish them? (*Of Fasting*).

Surely these are perfect examples of vigorous firmly-knit English, far nearer to the best models of today than the ambitious sermons of the seventeenth century, whether Anglican or Puritan.

Most of the discourses are made up of the common stock of Christianity. Being addressed to the general body of churchgoers, they keep to the high road of doctrine and practice as generally understood. *Against Peril of Idolatry*, however, is enormously long, closely reasoned, and crammed full of references to Scripture, the Fathers, and history generally. But the double method of proof, from the Bible and the Fathers, is characteristic of nearly all the Homilies. In particular, we note with interest the influence of the Old Testament upon the minds of the writers. The parallel between the godly reforming Kings of Judah, such as Hezekiah and Josiah, and " the Prince " of their own days is frequently drawn. Among the Fathers, St. Augustine's authority is paramount. Thus in *Concerning Prayer* we read: " But, admit the Saints do pray for us, yet do we not know how, whether specially for them which call upon them, or else generally for all men, wishing well to every man alike. If they pray specially for them which call upon them, then it is like they hear our prayers, and also know our heart's desire. Which thing to be false, it is already proved, both by the Scriptures, and also by the authority of Augustine." Prayers for the dead are treated in similar fashion. A loophole is left, though the practice is discouraged. The question is " whether we *ought* to pray for them that are departed out of this world, or no. Wherein if we will cleave only unto the word of God, then must we needs grant, that we have *no commandment* so to do." This is proved by the Parable of Dives and Lazarus, by other texts, and by the testimony of SS. Augustine, Cyprian, and Chrysostom.

The Holy Communion is described very beautifully (in *Concerning the Sacrament*) in phrases taken from " the ancient Catholic fathers " and " godly men ", as the salve of immortality, the pledge of eternal health, the defence of faith, the hope of the resurrection. We are urged " oftentimes to covet this bread, continually to thirst for this food ". " Look up with faith upon the holy Body and Blood of thy God, marvel with reverence, touch it with thy mind, receive it with thy hand, and take it fully with thy inward man."

There are two Sacraments only, " if they should be considered according to the exact signification of a Sacrament, namely, for visible signs expressly commanded in the New Testament, whereunto is annexed the promise of free forgiveness of our sin and of our holiness and joining in Christ ". " Absolution hath the promise of forgiveness of sin, yet by the express word of the New Testament it hath not this promise annexed and tied to the visible sign, which is imposition of hands."

The attitude towards the past is instructive. Superstition is repudiated, especially as regards the so-called holy things—" holy cowls, holy girdles, holy pardoned beads, holy shoes. . . ." (*Of Good Works*). Especially reprobated is " the blasphemous buying and selling the most precious Body and Blood of Christ in the mass " which has made the churches of England into dens of thieves " this many hundred years " (*For Repairing and Keeping Clean of Churches*). This abuse may be contrasted with the behaviour of " our godly predecessors " (*Of the Place and Time of Prayer*). There is no suggestion that a new Church was being set up, only that the old temple was being cleansed. Indeed the first twelve Homilies were put out before the First English Prayer Book and when no responsible person, probably, anticipated a final breach with Rome. It may be surmised that many of the Catholic-minded Churchmen who attended their parish churches in the early years of Elizabeth, and later became the separated Roman Catholic community, would have repudiated mediaeval abuses as heartily as the authors of the Homilies.

The incidental references to social conditions are very interesting. The bewilderment of simple folk at the changes is illustrated by what a woman said to her neighbour : ." Alas, gossip, what shall we now do at church, since all the saints are taken away, since all the goodly sights we were wont to have are gone, since we cannot hear the like piping, singing, chanting, and playing upon the organs, that we could before ? " (*Of the Place and Time of Prayer*). The moral chaos, a result of the Renaissance be it noted, not of the Reformation, which in 1547 had hardly had time to influence England, is described in *Against Whoredom and Uncleanness*. " This vice is grown into such a height, that in a manner among many it is counted no sin at all, but rather a pastime, a dalliance, and but a touch of youth ; not rebuked, but winked at ; not punished, but laughed at." This should be noted in view of the tendency to ascribe the laxity of the Elizabethan stage to the influence of the Reformation. " Of this vice ", proceeds the preacher, " cometh a great part of the divorces which nowadays be so commonly accustomed and used by man's private authority, to the great displeasure of God, and the breach of the most holy knot and bond of matrimony." This in a Homily set out by Henry VIII's authority ! It is remarkable that there is no defence of the Church such as is a commonplace today, as that the Church never allows divorce, but sometimes annuls a marriage. No, in Catholic England before the break with Rome, divorce is represented as common, arising from the husband's preferring a mistress, or the wife's preferring a lover, and resulting in the sin of adultery. " In what case are those adulterers which for the love of an whore put away their true and lawful wife against all law, right, reason, and conscience ? "

Wife-beating is condemned unsparingly. " If it be a great shame for a man to beat his bondservant (*i.e.*, maidservant), much more rebuke it is to lay violent hands upon his freewoman." Such a man, " if he may be called a man rather than a beast ", may be likened " to a killer of his father or his mother " (*Of the State of Matrimony*).

The Homily *Against Excess of Apparel* is amusing to modern readers. The Israelites were content to wear the same clothes and shoes for forty years (Deut. xxix. 5).

> But we are never contented, and therefore we prosper not ; so that most commonly he that ruffleth in his sables, in his fine furred gown, corked slippers, trim buskins, and warm mittons, is more ready to chill for cold than the poor labouring man, which can abide in the field all the day long, when the north wind blows, with a few beggarly clouts about him. We are loth to wear such as our fathers hath left us ; we think that not sufficient or good enough for us. We must have one gown for the day, another for the night ; one long, another short ; one for winter, another for summer ; one through furred, another but faced ; one for the working day, another for the holy day. . . .

If this witnesses to bygone conceptions of what luxury is, a little later a modern note is struck by the condemnation of women who paint their faces, dye and curl their hair, and " embalm " their bodies, on the pretext that they do it " to please our husband, to delight his eyes, and to retain his love toward us ".

A sidelight is thrown on the need for the strong, even tyrannical, Tudor Government, by the sermon *On Obedience*, which declares that without it " no man shall ride or go by the highway unrobbed ; no man shall sleep in his own house or bed unkilled ; no man shall keep his wife, children, and possessions in quietness ". The raw material of red revolution was present then just as it is now.

In Elizabeth's reign there was " great slackness and negligence of a great sort of people in resorting to the church ". Some came later, " scarcely at noon time "—so that services cannot have been always so early as some writers contend. Some behave so badly as to walk up and down the church all service time (*Of the Right Use of the Church*). Lastly let us quote two more illustrations of social conditions. In the *Sermon for Rogation Week* we are told of the bad custom of ploughing up part of the grass walks or balks between the cultivated strips of the common land. Decency dictates the leaving of at least " a broad and sufficient bierbalk to carry the corpse to the Christian sepulture ". Sometimes we hear the Elizabethan enforcing of fast days for the encouragement of the fisheries disparaged. But the Homily *Of Fasting* is quite explicit on the matter. The ordinance comes from the civil magistrate and is intended to help the coast towns by making a market for their fish, and thereby to strengthen the Navy, the burden of which then fell entirely on the ports ; also to lessen the demand for meat and so to bring down its price to the poor. It is explained that no religious sanction is imposed, other than the general duty of obeying the civil power. Not the religious fasts of the Church but the meatless days of the first world war form the true parallel.

When we are disheartened at reading a political history of the sixteenth century it is a tonic to turn to the vigorous exhortations to true religion, corporate as well as personal, contained in these famous but largely unread Homilies. The century was not so bad as it is the fashion to paint it nowadays.

VI

A SUFFOLK GRAMMAR SCHOOL

WHAT was life like in an English village in the days of Good Queen Anne ? In externals, of course, very different from what it is at the present day. But if we could go back seven or eight generations, we should probably find human nature pretty much the same as it is today. The clergyman would be seen quarrelling with the villagers, but yet making their interests his primary care ; in some places his ideas would be advanced enough to make him a founder of a Church school, for which he would solicit subscriptions from his neighbours. The farmers would be heard grumbling at the education provided, which only unfitted the lads for their station in life. Then, as now, the most sensitive part of a man would seem to have been his pocket, and consequently local assessment committees were wont to excite resentment by their vagaries.

Such, at least, is the conclusion I draw from an old document which reposes in a chest of papers belonging to the parish of Cavendish, in Suffolk. It is the report of a law-suit in the Court of Chancery in the year 1708, which possesses such vivid human interest, and throws such light on the manners of the time, that it deserves a better fate than oblivion amid a host of old leases and indentures.

The action was brought by James and Henry Grey, sons of the lately deceased Thomas Grey, Rector of Cavendish, together with a number of the inhabitants of the parish, against Edward Nevile and his wife Sarah, to recover some property which the latter were alleged to be occupying unlawfully. Thomas Grey, around whom the story revolves, had been Rector of Cavendish for more than fifty years. He was appointed towards the end of the Commonwealth, in 1657, when his name first appears in the registers as rector, though he was not instituted until 1661. In 1696 he founded a school, which was to be called after him and known as " Grey's Grammar School ", and endowed it with a small farm in the neighbouring parish of Pentlow, just over the Essex border. But it will be better to let the document tell its own tale.

The case for the plaintiffs comes first, representing the point of view of Dr. Grey's sons and the trustees of the school. The spelling is left untouched, but the frequent abbreviations are written out in full.

Dr. Thomas Grey, say the plaintiffs,

> had throughout the whole course of his residence among them received
> continuall proofes of their affection and esteem and being very much
> increased in his worldly state and fortune had upon all occasions ex-
> pressed the sense he had of such their kindness and appeared very
> desirous by some public and beneficial act of charity to perpetuate those
> his friendly dispositions and that to that intent and purpose he had
> frequently consulted with several of the chief inhabitants

of the place as to the best method of doing so. At their request he
purchased a house, which he fitted up as a school, and installed a
master therein. For an endowment he bought from Henry Kemp,
the squire of Pentlow, a farm of eighty acres, for which the tenant,
Edward Nice, paid a rent of £25. In 1696 he settled the whole
property on trustees for the benefit of the school. The school
flourished, and everybody, including the founder, was pleased.

However, in 1702 a change came over the scene. The rector was
now more than eighty years old, " very infirm in body and visibly
deranged and impaired in the faculties of his mind and unable to
manage himself and his concerns with that care as he was wont to
do ". Taking advantage of his weakness,

> the defendant Sarah Nevile then Sarah Wright . . . used all imaginable
> application and industry to be received into his family as an house-
> keeper and she succeeded therein. She had endeavoured by various
> indirect and insinuating arts to get the ascendant over him the said Thomas
> Grey who dayly declined in his understanding by which means she
> occasioned great disorder and confusion among his dearest friends which
> ended in a general separation from his house and company and would
> not suffer him to be easy till he altered his will . . . and procured him
> to sign another.

Soon afterwards the old man died, and the inhabitants expected
to enjoy the benefits of his foundation, but Sarah Wright, who
now became Mrs. Nevile, went to live on the farm, alleging that it
had been left to her in the final will, which annulled all previous
arrangements. After her death, so she declared, it was to go to the
Rector of Cavendish and the Vicar of Wickhambrook, a neighbouring village, with their respective churchwardens in equal shares, with
a view to being distributed to the deserving poor of the two parishes.
The plaintiffs prayed the court to compel the defendants, with whom
the vicar and churchwardens of Wickhambrook were associated, to
deliver up the property to its rightful owners.

The plaintiffs' case sounds overwhelmingly strong, and we are
curious to hear what defence the opposition could make. Of course,

no will could annul a properly executed deed of conveyance, and it was on this point that the court's decision turned. But the defendants, if not able to win the day, at least succeeded in showing that the picture of a model parish presided over by a benevolent and beloved, if somewhat senile, rector, was very wide of the mark.

The defendants, in their reply, admitted many of the facts, but declared that they " did not believe that Thomas Grey did throughout the whole course of his residence among the inhabitants of the said parish receive continued proofes of their good affection and esteem. . . . On the contrary they had been informed and believe the said parish did not well esteem him but disobliged him very often so that he had perpetuated his resentment of their unkindness and ingratitude towards him by his last will dated the twenty sixth of July 1702." It was true that Thomas Grey intended founding a charity, and purchased some property with a view to a settlement, but they had no knowledge of any such settlement being carried out. They believed that the schoolmaster received a salary, but was not actually in possession of any house or land.

At this point extracts from the will were read, some of which we reproduce here:

" I give and bequeath unto Mrs Sarah Wright the niece of my loving wife and now my housekeeper and to her assignes all those pieces of land [the estate at Pentlow is now specified] " . . . After her death it was to go " unto the poor people of Cavendish where I now still through the goodwill and patience of my Lord God continue rector and to the poor people of Wickambrooke where I was for some time vicar ". The rent was to be divided between the two incumbents on the Feast of St. Thomas the Apostle at the sign of the White Horse, but if it ever should be pulled down, then at the rector's house at Cavendish. The Vicar of Wickambrook was to have ten shillings over and above his share in order to defray the cost of his journey. The distribution must be made " wisely and faithfully . . . as long as the world continues ", and special respect should be paid " to the honest godly sober and diligent poor and such as have the greatest burthen of children sickness and old age ". A copy of the will was to be kept " to the end of the world . . . in the town chest ".

I had erected a school house [continues the will] and furnished it within with a very convenient desk for the master of the scholars . . . but the inhabitants proving altogether ungrateful, some slighting my kindness saying they needed not so much but an ordinary schoolmaster to teach and instruct their children such a one as could write and read and cast accounts, now for these reasons so annoying me for what I had done and discovering their spite [at last we get to the real cause of all the trouble] by advancing and raising the Rectory in the public taxes to over £100 now raised to £160 reduced to £120 now raised to £160 again so that I am now compelled for nothing provokes me more than ingratitude to dispose of the said endowments . . . to other charitable purposes.

After the reading of the will various witnesses were called. Sarah Nevile declared that Thomas Grey wrote to her in 1701 imploring her to come and live with him as housekeeper, which she did. She had always tried to preserve peace in the family circle, and it was through no fault of hers that the children left home. Edward Nevile said that he married in May, 1706, and corroborated his wife's testimony. He upheld her claim to the farm, but disclaimed any right in the school buildings. John Cowper, Vicar of Wickambrook, was called next. He remembered going to see Thomas Grey in 1701 to ask for " some voluntary contribution to the said town of Wickambrooke towards teaching poor children of Wickambrooke aforesaid to read ". Dr. Grey gave him a favourable reception, and promised twenty shillings a quarter towards this object. It was on this occasion that he showed him the will and read out the clause according to which the Vicar of Wickhambrook should ultimately have half of the Pentlow estate. After the death of the testator the witness went to Henry Grey, who had succeeded his father in the Rectory of Cavendish, and inquired about the will, but could get no satisfaction. Finally the trustees were called, who declared that they had never heard of the will before the preceding Christmas.

The case was heard on July 14th, 1708, and lasted a long time. At last when all the documents had been produced and read, including the deed of purchase dated 1696, it was by " the right honble William Lord Cowper Baron of Wingham Lord High Chancellor of Great Brittain and by the power and authority of the said high and honble Court of Chancery Ordered and Decreed " that the lands were to go to the purposes of the deed and not to follow the dispositions of the will ; also that the Neviles were to give account for all the rents they had received, and that the costs were to be refunded to the plaintiffs out of the charity.

No other verdict was possible ; and yet we feel sorry for the poor old rector, who was the sole source of all the benefits. With great generosity he had parted with a large sum of money in his lifetime

G

in order to improve the village. In return the villagers exercised their time-honoured prerogative of grumbling. Why had he made such a fuss over his school ? A worse one would have done for them ! Then no doubt the farmers had reflected that if he could part with so much money, he must be wealthy, and therefore could afford to pay a larger share of the rates of the parish. The old man was cut to the quick, and so made the last will in which he tried to divert the money to other charitable uses and associated his old parish with Cavendish. He had been rector of the latter for some fifty years, but, at the last, memories of his first parish and happy times spent there revived, and he intended, if possible, to put it on an equality with the village which had been to him a source of disillusion and disappointment.

So Dr. Grey went in peace to his grave underneath the altar of Cavendish church. The church stands at the top of the village green, and at the bottom is a long, low building which is now a dwelling-house, but which for two hundred years bore the name of " Grey's Grammar School ". Alas for the vanity of human wishes, at least when they are those of charitable testators ! In 1907 this foundation, instituted in 1696, that is, when the present divisions of English religion already existed, and endowed out of the private purse of the parish clergyman as a home of Church teaching for ever, was closed by order of the Board of Education, and its money diverted to purely secular objects.

If the charity as originally designed did not go on " to the end of the world ", no more did the inn of the White Horse referred to in the will. Its demise was to be expected in the course of time, but it was a strange coincidence that it was closed in accordance with the decrees of the licensing authority in 1908, the year following the school, and was pulled down soon afterwards.

VII

PATRICK GORDON AND HIS GEOGRAPHY

Geography Anatomiz'd or The Geographical Grammar [1] is a book of great charm. It was published in 1693 and went through twenty editions, the last in 1754. The author, Patrick Gordon, a naval chaplain and Fellow of the Royal Society, one of the first two missionaries of the S.P.G., deserves a niche in the temple of fame by the side of Dr. Bray; he went to America in 1702 and died the same year. As we shall see, his book was apparently the first attempt to arouse interest in Missions among the members of the Church of England.

The Preface states that the book " is principally design'd for the use and benefit of the younger sort of our nobility and gentry ", who for want of occupation are led away by gross immoralities. History is indeed a proper study for gentlemen, but geography is a necessary introduction to modern history. By 1701 the book had been adopted by " many of our publick schools "; it contains about 200,000 words, and has a number of maps, " for ornament not for use ".

It begins with forty-eight Problems (to which answers are provided) by which the appetite of the scholars may be whetted. The use of the globe is assumed. Problem 11 runs: " To know by the globe when the Great Mogul of India, and Czar of Moscov sit down to dinner—supposing withal that mid-day in the afo said cities is dining-time ". He refrains from proving that t' earth is round, for that is rarely doubted " except it be by men and children ".

The main part of the book is extraordinarily accurate, in view of the difficulty the author must have experienced in getting information. But before reaching it he has a section of " Geographical Paradoxes ", which is nothing but a collection of tall stories that he has heard from sailors. Thus No. 3 : " There is a certain place of the earth, at which if two men should chance to meet, one would stand upright upon the soles of the other's feet, and neither of them should feel the other's weight, and yet both should retain their natural

[1] My copy was given me about 1915 by Edward Conybeare, formerly Vicar of Barrington, near Cambridge. The first and last pages are lost, but after some research Mr. Conybeare reconstructed the history of the book as given above, and provided a summary of what is missing.

posture." And No. 31 : " There is a certain country in South
America, many of whose savage inhabitants are such unheard of
canibals, that they not only feed upon human flesh, but also some
of them do actually eat *themselves*, and yet they commonly survive
that strange repast." " The unmasking of them [these Paradoxes]
may prove a private diversion, both pleasant and useful to the
ingenious reader, at his more vacant times."

Each country of the globe is then treated in turn, under a uniform
system of heads, including " Rarities, Archbishopricks, Bishopricks,
Universities, Manners etc ". Thus we have " Tartary. Archbishopricks, Bishopricks, Universities, none ". Every language
spoken in the chief European countries is illustrated by the Lord's
Prayer. Germany includes Holland and Belgium ; Prussia appears
as the Mark of Brandenburgh, in the Circle of Upper Saxony.
Turkey includes Hungary, Croatia, the Crimea, and of course the
Balkans and Greece, with a note that Hungary is now almost entirely
under the Emperor.

The characterization of the nations reflects British prejudices
as well as historical facts. Sweden has become terrible to other
nations. The Danes are so vain " that upon almost every under-
taking of their King and country do they use to strike medals ;
and such as express the action done in a most *hyperbolical* manner,
tho' sometimes the matter in it self ' of so small importance, that no
nation of *Europe*, but the *Danish*, would hardly deem it worthy of
a place in their weekly *Gazette* ". The French are " airy, amorous,
full of action, compleat masters of the art of dissimulation ", but
are renowned for their learning. No part of Christendom is less
religious than Holland. The Poles are remarkable for their fluent
speaking of Latin. The Italians are less given to the art of war
than most other nations ; they " are generally reputed a grave,
respectful and ingenious sort of people ".

After describing the Continent Gordon proceeds to the islanders,
beginning with Great Britain. The Scots are highly praised. They
are frugal, " chusing rather to improve the mind, than pamper the
body " ; and virtuous—" many abominable vices, too common in
other countries, are not so much as speculatively known in 'em ".

And what of the English ? They are an admirable admixture
of Northern and Southern characteristics ; " ingenious and active,
yet solid and persevering. . . . No nation hath yet surpassed the
English, and none can justly pretend to equal them." " Of such

an admirable Constitution is the English Government, that no nation whatsoever can justly pretend to such a model, and no people in the world may live more happy if they please. . . .

O fortunatos nimium, sua si bona norint, Anglicanos."

The description of England is interesting. The land has two chief lakes—Winandermere, and Whittlemere, in Huntingdonshire. It is so fertile that it is known as " the granary of the Western world ". It has two Universities, the colleges of which are equal in importance to some foreign Universities. The antiquities are notable, especially Stonehenge. As for religion, in their Reformation the inhabitants " were not so hurry'd by popular fury and faction (as in other nations) but proceeded in a more prudent, regular, and Christian method ; resolving to separate no further from the Church of Rome than she had separated from the truth . . . so that the Reform'd Church of England is a true mean or middle way between those two ex-treames, of superstition and phanaticism, both equally to be avoided. . . . The Church of England doth firmly hold and maintain the whole body of the Catholic faith (and none other) according to Holy Scripture, and the four first General Councils."

Mr. Gordon is less complimentary to the Celtic fringe. The Welsh " (at least the most intelligent of 'em) are of the Reform'd religion, according to the platform of the Church of England ; but many of the meaner sort are so grossly ignorant in religious matters, that they differ nothing from mere heathens ". The Scots, though praised on the whole, as we have seen, suffer from " lamentable distractions ", and fatal " heats and divisions ".

Coming to Asia and Africa, we are surprised to find the wealth of information about such countries as Burma, the Moluccas, and Madagascar. The accounts of these continents are given with reserve, " our intelligence of 'em being as yet very slender ", but with a good deal of detail, drawn from the best travellers' tales. Geography has lost much in romance by gaining in accuracy. But Turkey in Asia with its ruins of a mighty civilization (" *quaeque ipse miserrima vidi* ") is described from the naval chaplain's personal observation.

Reaching America, Gordon warms to his work and writes with even more gusto. Each of the North American Colonies is treated separately. Of Jamaica he writes : " The inhabitants of this island are of the same religion with that publickly profess'd, and by law established in England; excepting the Negroe-slaves, who (both here, and in other islands of the English Plantations) are still kept in woful ignorance; which is undoubtedly a grievous scandal to our holy profession in general, and an abominable shame to their respective masters in particular. But let such masters know, that the time is coming, when the (now) despised souls of those toiling slaves will certainly be requir'd at their hands." A similar statement is made about Barbados, where the planters are said to believe that a slave when baptized ceases to be a slave, and therefore to oppose conversions.

The conclusion of the book gives an account of all the European plantations in Asia, Africa and America, and puts forward proposals " for the Propagation of the blessed Gospel in all pagan countries ". Gordon points out that only one-sixth of the world professes Christianity. The English have great responsibilities for the Plantations. He proposes that they should fulfil them as follows. Every freeholder to subscribe a five-hundredth part of his income; the merchants of London a two-hundredth part; the clergy a hundredth part. This sum, if invested, would produce an income sufficient to send a band of missionaries. The chief languages of the areas to be evangelized will have to be learned in England; but where the multitude of dialects spoken by few people makes the difficulty insoluble the natives will have to learn English. He particularly urges the planters of North America not to " extirpate the Paynim " but to convert them. " It is far more honourable to overcome paganism in one than to destroy 1000 pagans. Every convert is a conquest."

It is this strong missionary fervour that justifies the inclusion here of a notice of a forgotten book. Patrick Gordon must have contributed greatly to the stirring of conscience which led to the foundation of the S.P.C.K. and the S.P.G.

Every page of the book can be read with pleasure and profit. Its wise and witty, truly Christian and apostolically minded, author must have been one of the finest products of Anglicanism, and we long to know more about him. The S.P.C.K. records give a fleeting glimpse. On Dec. 16th, 1700, he was elected " Correspondent for the Navy ". He formulated plans for " the Christian instruction of seamen ", which were deemed impracticable. On Feb. 22nd, 1700/1, he wrote (as summarized) : " As to the reformation of the seamen, he recommends the gift of a little tobacco to be join'd to good advice and instruction; which being done with a due air of

measure reviv'd ; in such a manner, at least, as not to give the occasion we now have, every Ash-Wednesday, to lament its loss or decay among us.

How far this " Way of Renewal " was a spiritual force it would be hard to say. At least it is a proof of the earnestness and good sense of the times. But the library scheme took root very soon in most dioceses.

At last on December 16th, 1699, he sailed for Maryland, borrowing money and selling his personal belongings to pay his passage. He arrived on March 12th and set to work to get the delayed Bill for establishing the Church through the Assembly. With some difficulty, owing to " the insinuations of the *Quakers* and *Papists* (no unnatural coalition) ", he succeeded. On May 22nd, 1704, he held a general visitation of the clergy of the province at Annapolis. The Assembly and the clergy agreed in wishing him to return home and secure the Royal Assent to the Bill of Establishment, which was by no means certain.

Back in London, Dr. Bray had to face great opposition from influential Quakers.

> But the Doctor refuted their specious objections by unanswerable reasons, and placed the affair in such an advantageous light, that His Majesty decided, without any appearance of hesitation, in the Church's favour, and gave the Royal Assent in these remarkable words : *Have the Quakers the benefit of a toleration?   Let the Establish'd Church have an establish'd maintenance.*

We hasten through the concluding years of this useful life. In 1706 Dr. Bray accepted the Rectory of St. Botolph Without. In 1712 he published his *Martyrology*, or *Papal Usurpation*, a successor to which book was never completed. However, his materials were bequeathed to Sion College. He began training young clergymen to be missionaries to the negroes on the Plantations. Among other books, he published his *Directorium Missionarium* in 1726, and reprinted Erasmus' *Ecclesiastes*, which he particularly admired. In 1727 he began visiting Whitechapel prison. The conditions were appalling : he raised funds to supply the prisoners with bread, beef, and broth on Sundays ; arranged for spiritual ministrations, which were given by his missionaries in training, " to inure them to the most distasteful parts of their office " ; and made known " the sore . . . and . . . inhumanity . . . which, afterwards some worthy patriots of the House of Commons, took so much pains to enquire into and redress ".

" Being now far advanced in years, and continually reminded of his approaching change, by the imbecility and decays of old age ", he took steps to increase the number of the Associates (of Dr. Bray's Libraries), enlisting the services of General Oglethorpe, the famous founder of Georgia. A plan for emigrating young people i work-houses to America seems to have failed. But Dr. Bray to k the leading part in establishing the Society for Reformation of Mar iers, in setting up Charity Schools, and in the affairs of the Society foi the Relief of Poor Proselytes. " Most of the Religious Societies in London owe grateful acknowledgments to his memory, and are in i great measure formed on the plans he projected."

At this point the narrator lets himself go and ends on a high resounding eighteenth century note.

> And now the Doctor having happily lodged his principal designs in the hands of able managers, being on the verge of the grave, he could not but review his undertakings with complacency, and thank the good providence of God, which appeared, to lay such trains for their advancement. His conscience crown'd him with a secret applause, which was an inexhaustible source of comfortable reflections and joyful presages in his last minutes.

It is easy to smile and to recall the pompous epitaphs on the tombs of bewigged divines. But the words at least prove to a less unsophisticated generation that Thomas Bray believed that God " is, and that he is a rewarder of them that seek him ". Without this two-fold belief we fight a losing battle against the insurgent forces of " humanism ". Human nature needs an adequate motive to sustain it in a life-long struggle. We need not be ashamed of " joyful presages " of a heavenly reward, for the reward can only be spiritual. Those who affect to despise it are alien in spirit to the heroes of faith who answered the roll call in the eleventh chapter of the Hebrews, and, like Moses, " looked unto the recompense of reward ".

IX

GEORGE HORNE, WILLIAM JONES, AND WILLIAM STEVENS

SIR MAX BEERBOHM, in a wonderful little essay entitled " A Clergyman ", after quoting Dr. Johnson's words, recorded by Boswell under April 7th, 1778, regarding certain divines—South, Seed, Jortin, Smalridge—asks : " And, by the way, who *were* they, these worthies ? It is a solemn thought that so little is conveyed to us by names which to the palaeo-Georgians conveyed so much. We discern a dim, composite figure of a big man in a big wig and a billowing black gown, with a big congregation beneath him. But we are not anxious to hear what he is saying."

This pretty well expressed my feelings about the shadowy figure of " Jones of Nayland ", who appears in Church histories as a precursor of the Oxford Movement. However, one day I picked up the Life of William Stevens and was so much interested that I went on to read his Life of William Jones, printed in his edition of the Works of William Jones, twelve volumes in all.[1] And Jones' Works contain a Life of Horne. The three friends began to stand out as a group deserving attention. Further study revealed a cross-section of eighteenth century life—the episcopate, biblical scholarship, Oxford University, science, country parsons, controversy, business, Church administration, practical charity—and I was very much interested to hear what they had to say.

In their day they were associated by the public as Hutchinsonians, an epithet which recalls a forgotten controversy. John Hutchinson (1674–1737) [2] was famous in his day for a system of biblical philosophy, treated most fully in his book *Moses's Principia*, in which he opposed Newton's *Principia*. Hebrew, he held, was the primitive language ; in which the whole of revelation was concealed. The consonants (not the vowel points and accents, which are human additions) interpreted mystically give the clue to the interpretation of all knowledge, whether natural or spiritual. In its later form

---

[1] How completely Jones has been forgotten I realized when I cut the pages of several volumes of the series in the library of Sion College, London. They were a presentation set, given soon after publication.

[2] Steward to the Duke of Somerset, to whose doctor, John Woodward, he gave his collection of fossils, which formed the nucleus of the Woodwardian collection at Cambridge. Hutchinson's Collected Works were published in 12 volumes in 1753.

his teaching was strongly opposed to the natural religion which was becoming fashionable, and insisted on the necessity of revelation. His followers took up this part of his teaching, discarding some of his eccentricities.

Overton and Relton in their standard history of the Church of England in the eighteenth century mention Horne, Jones, and Stevens, in the same breath as Butler, Secker, and Benson. They associate Stevens with even more famous names. "A period which produced . . . such lay Churchmen as Edmund Burke and Samuel Johnson, William Wilberforce and William Stevens, must have been at any rate a period worth studying." [1]

(a) GEORGE HORNE

Let us take George Horne first, as a bishop, though perhaps to us the least interesting of the three. Our information is derived from the biography by William Jones, who in the preface to the second edition (1799) writes: "In publishing the Memoirs of the Life of Bishop Horne my intention was only to give a true idea of that good man, as it presented itself to my memory and affections; and to produce an edifying book, rather than a formal history." He proceeds to define the sense in which Horne and he are Hutchinsonians.

"The followers of Mr. Hutchinson give to *God* the pre-eminence in every thing." "They hold, that only one way of salvation has been revealed to man from the foundation of the world." Divine things are explained by the natural creation. They are Trinitarians, kept such by their principles, especially by "the Hutchinsonian philosophy of fire, light, and air". They derive everything from revelation, not from the natural powers of man. They emphasize the types and figures of Scripture. They object to Newton's method of proving a vacuum. They believe in a universal flood, and diligently collect fossils to prove it. They look with suspicion on heathen books, do not trust Jews as expositors of the Bible, and believe Hebrew to have been the original language. These tenets, he concludes, revived "the dying flame of Christian faith . . . in Bishop Horne and myself".

George Horne (1730–92) was the son of Samuel Horne, the Rector of Otham, Kent, and one of seven children. His father was of a mild and gentle temper. "When his son George was an infant, he

[1] *A History of the English Church*, ed. by Stephens and Hunt, VII. 1.

used to wake him with playing upon a flute, that the change from
sleeping to waking might be gradual and pleasant, and not produce
an outcry." George was taught by his father till the age of thirteen,
when he was sent to the Grammar School at Maidstone. The
Master, the Rev. Deodatus Bye, was " a man of good principles,
and well learned in Latin, Greek and Hebrew ".[1] " There was
another boy . . . of whom the master was heard to say, that he
never did anything which he wished him not to have done." [2] At
fifteen, having learned some Hebrew as well as the classics, Horne
went to University College, Oxford, with a Maidstone scholarship,
along with William Jones, who became his lifelong friend. Later
he was elected a Kentish Fellow of Magdalen, there being no native
of Kent among the scholars of that College. He ánd Jones
joined a group which was interested in Hebrew and fossils. They
were introduced to Hutchinson's writings by a gentleman (George
Watson) who studied them but kept them to himself—" Why,
these things are in no repute, the world does not receive them ".
Horne's convictions were formed after Jones left Oxford. " The
system of Divinity in the Holy Scriptures is explained and attested
by the scriptural account of created Nature." Divines who extol
the dignity of human nature do much harm. The University
teaches ethics and philosophy rather than divinity and is in danger
substituting the Stoic *anima mundi* for the Christian God.

Horne's first publication was an anonymous pamphlet on the
Newtonian philosophy. In 1760 he published *A View of Mr
Kennicott's Method of correcting the Hebrew Text*, which he judged
unfavourably. Jeremy Taylor was one of his favourite authors ;
another was William Law, to whose rules of devotion he conformed
in many respects, though rejecting his mysticism.

As a young man Horne was very handsome, though short-sighted.
He took no athletic exercise. He married a daughter of Philip
Burton, by whom he had three daughters. In 1768 he became
President of Magdalen, in 1781 Dean of Canterbury, and in 1791
Bishop of Norwich. His health was poor in later years and he used
to visit Brighton and Ramsgate for the sea-bathing.

When he was Dean of Canterbury he concerned himself with the
application of the Scottish Bishops for relief, in association with
Jones and Stevens.[3] On a hill near Canterbury he said one day .

[1] Bye took his B.A. at Oxford (All Souls) in 1718 and relinquished the
Maidstone post in 1746.
[2] William Stevens, Horne's cousin.
[3] See below, under Stevens.

" If the great Apostle of the Gentiles were upon earth, and it were put to his choice with what denomination of Christians he would communicate, the preference would probably be given to the Episcopalians of Scotland, as most like to the people he had been used to."

Little is recorded of his brief episcopate, other than his refusal to interfere with John Wesley's activities, " if the minister of the parish made no objection ". His treatment of an infringement of copyright shows magnanimity. John Wesley " sold a work of mine, as if it had been an original work, partly copied, and partly put into English verse, without asking the consent, or making a word of acknowledgment, in the Title or a Preface, to the author. He was free to produce any possible good from any labour of mine, without being envied." Add to this magnanimity that he was lavish in his charities and saved nothing from his ecclesiastical preferments, and we have a picture of a man whose goodness justified the reputation he enjoyed.

His great work was *A Commentary on the Book of Psalms*, begun in 1758 and finished in 1776, which reached its tenth edition in 1816, and in an abridged edition continued to be circulated by the S.P.C.K. until about the middle of the nineteenth century. This is a learned work in its way, though the notes on Hebrew matters seem to depend on Lowth. It is intended " for them that believe ". The guiding principle of the exposition sounds less unscholar than it would have done a generation ago, namely that the way the Psalms are quoted in the New Testament shows how the other Psalms, which are not quoted, are to be interpreted. The tablets to his memory in Norwich Cathedral and in the village church of Elham, Kent, referred to this work. " His Commentary on the Psalms will continue to be a Companion to the Closet until the Devotion of Earth shall end in the Hallelujahs of Heaven."

In his day he had a great reputation as a preacher. To the modern reader his *Discourses on Several Subjects and Occasions*, in four volumes, seem rather flat and uninteresting, largely because they are completely devoid of anything that throws light on contemporary history or manners. But it is no small feat to have preached many sermons, mostly to the University of Oxford, which, suitably abridged, could be preached today to an average congregation—to their profit, though not to the glory of the preacher. William Jones in his " Prefatory Epistle [to the Life] to William Stevens Esq." says : " You . . . may guess how refined his raptures were."

By refinement he probably meant a scrupulous adherence to a balanced statement of truth and an avoidance of rhetorical passages. It is a tribute to the University that it listened patiently to plain teaching such as we might describe as being " on the Sunday School level ".   The goodness of a man whose life of devotion was modelled on the rules of William Law must have added impressiveness to somewhat ordinary discourses.   One sermon was preached from the open-air pulpit of Magdalen College on St. John Baptist's Day, 1755.   A footnote says : " The Quadrangle was furnished round the sides with a large fence of green boughs, that the preaching might more nearly resemble that of John the Baptist. . . . For many years the custom hath been discontinued."

In a Preface Dr. Horne remarks on the changed taste of the age. " Thousands received instruction and consolation formerly fro. . sermons, which would not now be endured. . . . The next [century] will behold a set of writers of a fashion suited to it, when our discourses shall in their turn, be antiquated and forgotten among men." [1]   He has aimed at simplicity.   " I have done as well as I could ; and know not that it will be in my power to do better. Nobler and more extensive ideas rise before me ; but planning and executing are very different things. . . . Accept such as I give, and pardon errors and imperfections.

" I stand at the door of the temple, with my torch.   If you would view it's glories, enter in, and there dwell for ever."

A good specimen of the more learned among the sermons is one of 1769 on " The Word Incarnate ".   The derivation of the Word in St. John's Prologue from Heraclitus, Philo etc., is discussed and rejected.   The source of the phrase is to be found in the Old Testament and the Targum ; God's Word is thought communicated in speech ; the flesh means the whole man.   The sermon ends with a simple exposition of the Catholic doctrine as against the errors of Arius, Apollinaris, Nestorius and Eutyches.   If a modern orthodox preacher chose the subject at all, he would not wish to treat it differently.

Lastly let me mention a piece of popular controversy in a different vein : *A Letter to Dr. Adam Smith on the Life, Death, and Philosophy of his friend, David Hume Esq.*   Hume died in 1776 and his autobiography, edited by Adam Smith, appeared in 1777.   It contains a lucid summary of Hume's views, which are allowed to speak for

---

[1] Note the contrast between the panegyric on the monument and the modesty of the author.

H

themselves, introduced by an urbane and brightly written exposure of the damaging effect upon religion of the writings of a man whom Dr. Smith described " as approaching as nearly to the idea of a perfectly wise and virtuous man, as perhaps the nature of human frailty will permit ".[1] It is sufficient to quote a few passages which throw light on Horne's character. " Trust me, good Loctor, I am no bigot, enthusiast, or enemy to human learning—*Et ego in Arcadia* —I have made many a hearty meal, in private, upon Cicero and Virgil, as well as Mr Hume. . . . I never knew what envy or hatred was ; and am ready, at all times, to praise, wherever I can do it in honour and conscience. . . . Friend as I am to freedom of opinion (and no one living can be more so) . . ."

(b) WILLIAM JONES

The Theological, Philosophical and Miscellaneous Works of the Rev. William Jones, M.A., F.R.S., edited by William Stevens, were collected and published in twelve volumes in 1801. The list of subscribers, printed at the beginning of the first volume, shows that 342 sets were subscribed, including eight sets taken by the Archbishop of Canterbury. Stevens' lively biography of his friend prefixed to the first volume illustrates admirably the career of an exemplary eighteenth century priest.

Jones was born at Lowick in Northants in 1726, of a Welsh father. An ancestor was Colonel Jones, who married Oliver Cromwell's sister, and as a lad William felt the guilt of regicide resting on him personally. His industry was unwearied and he was nominated to a scholarship at Charterhouse, from which school at the age of eighteen he went to University College, Oxford ; there he read Hutchinson's writings and made a friend of George Horne.

In 1751 he was ordained priest by the Bishop of Lincoln, his curacy being at Finedon, in his native county. In 1753 he published his first book, a *Full Answer* to Bishop Clayton's *Essay on Spirit*, in which his characteristic teaching appeared. The Trinity, he maintained, acknowledged by pagan nations was not " a Trinity in the divine nature " ; image-worship derived from the cherubic figures set up at the east of the Garden of Eden. In 1754 he compiled *The Catholic Doctrine of the Trinity* and engaged in scientific experiments, towards the expenses of which his friends subscribed £300 a year for three years. When the first volume of his *Essay*

[1] A new edition of the pamphlet was published by the S.P.C.K. as late as 1840.

on the First Principles of Natural Philosophy appeared in 1762, the Earl of Bute instructed Mr. Adams, the mathematical instrument maker, to supply him with all the instruments he wanted.

" It was said that ' no one remembered the poor wise man who saved the city ', but the Author of *The Catholic Doctrine of the Trinity*, who did such eminent service for the City of God, was not forgotten ; he was remembered by Archbishop Secker, who presented him ; first to the Vicarage of Bethersden in Kent, in the year 1764, and soon after to the more valuable Rectory of Pluckley in the same county, as some reward for his able defence of Christian Orthodoxy." So writes Stevens, who says that Archbishop Secker's prejudices against Hutchinsonianism " must have been greatly done away before he became the patron of Mr. Jones ". When the Essay on Natural Philosophy was published the Archbishop said : " If it is not answered, we little folks shall infer, that it cannot be answered." " And it never was answered ", adds Stevens.

After twelve years Jones went to Nayland, from which Suffolk village he derived his usual description. He seems to have been a model parish priest. Finding very few communicants at first, by incessant labours in the pulpit and out of it he succeeded in getting the sacrament well attended. He was an assiduous teacher, instructing the children privately in his house and publicly in the church, and being " the sole Sunday Schoolmaster " ; to help his parishioners he had learned medicine as a young man ; a competent musician, he improved the music of his church. All the time he played his part in current Church affairs and kept up to date with the science of his day.

In 1799 his wife, who had formed her mind on the pattern of Jeremy Taylor's *Holy Living and Holy Dying*, died, and he had a stroke. Soon after this came his own last illness, during which the sacrament was frequently administered to him. " If this be dying, Mr. Sims," he said to his curate, " I had no idea what dying was before." In the Life of Stevens, described in the next section, a letter is printed from a neighbouring clergyman. " On the morning of the Epiphany [1800], that good and wise man was conducted to the presence of that Saviour in whom he trusted, and the fruition of the three Persons in the Eternal Godhead, whose doctrine he maintained upon earth with so much ability and conviction."

" Greatly as he loved his family," says Stevens, " no interest occupied so much of his attention in his latter days, as that of Christ and his Church ; and the danger to which she is exposed, under the present circumstances of the Christian world, [was] amongst the heaviest of the afflictions which he endured."

We now turn to his literary remains, which fill twelve volumes and include theological essays, catechetical material, scientific treatises, sermons, and much else. Everything is lucid, sensible, well expressed:[1] nothing goes deeply into the problems, and for this reason the writings are important, as giving expression to the common views of orthodox Churchmen. Their great preoccupation is with the fashionable tenets of natural religion. " O fatal day for England ! when the *religion of nature* . . . first gained admission into lecture-books . . . now too firmly established to be shaken by such a hand as mine." " O learned Andrewes ; O blessed Kenn ; O holy Beveridge ; O wise and sagacious Leslie ; your days are past ! " (*Sermons*, XII). Natural religion is represented as the original religion of reason and nature, Christianity as the superstructure. Every man is his own priest, his own temple, so the priesthood of Christ is rejected ; so is the doctrine of the corruption of man's nature (*An Essay on the Church*, IV). " If there is a doctrine among Christians, which can render their whole creed ineffectual and impertinent, it is this, that *religion* . . . is *natural* to man " (*An Essay on Man*, VII, 297).

The work by which Jones became known to posterity, *The Catholic Doctrine of the Trinity*, must be judged by the conditions of contemporary controversy. The massive patristic learning of the seventeenth century had almost disappeared ; or at least it was considered irrelevant. The Church was confronted by a movement which reopened the Arian controversy. The arguments of the fourth century were no longer applicable, the day of the critical treatment of the Bible had not dawned—both sides accepted the Bible as the court of appeal. So Jones, like other writers of his time, set out to prove, by a catena of texts, that the Bible teaches Trinitarianism. St. Paul speaks of " the day of Christ " and " the day of God " indifferently, therefore Christ is God. The Spirit is in Christians, God is in Christians ; Ananias lies to the Holy Ghost, and to God— therefore the Spirit is God. To some modern readers the method may seem ingenuous, but it served its purpose and this particular line of attack has not been reopened. If his opponents relied ostensibly on the Bible, their motive power was the fashionable

---

[1] It is interesting to notice a sentence like " This doctrine favors the practise . . .", in which so cultured and popular a writer uses " American spelling ". See *Works*, VII. 13. (Quotations will generally give the volume and title of the treatise.)

doctrine that we all worship the same God, as in Pope's " Universal
Prayer ".   " All that can be known of the true God, is to be known
by *Revelation* " (I. xcii).   So much does Jones insist on this that he
classes Deists, " Quakers, Methodists, and particularly the Rev.
Mr. William Law as opposers of revelation ", owing to their doctrine
of the inner light (I. xcvii).   No doubt he would have considered his
later work, *A Short Way to Truth, or The Christian Doctrine of the
Trinity in Unity* (1792), a more scientific treatment of the subject.
The Trinity is there proved from the analogy of nature —the three
primary colours ; length, breadth and height ; the three principles
of motion seen in fire, light and air ; or heart, lungs and nerves in
man.

In one of his sermons Jones says : " I end as I began : I say,
Hear the Church." In a *Letter to a Young Gentleman at Oxford,
intended for Holy Orders,* he speaks of " the Church of England still
preserving in it an apostolical succession of government, together
with a plan of unadulterated Christian doctrine, the nearest of any
upon earth to the apostolical and primitive pattern " (I. 260).   He
had no illusions about the actual state of the Church.   " If we look
at our own Church, we have but a melancholy prospect ; and cannot
help observing that it approximates too near to the state of the Jewish
Church before its destruction " (*An Essay on the Church*, IV. 454).
The Temple as a den of thieves reappears in the sale of advowsons,
" which is too far gone to be reformed, and too bold to be censured "
(IV. 456).   " But whatever abuses there may be in the Church,
it is our duty to make the best of it.   The Church is our spiritual
mother ; and we may apply those words of the wise man, *despise
not thy mother when she is old* ; not even if she should be in rags and
dotage.   The doctrine of the Church of England is, by profession,
still pure and apostolical ; and, whatever faults it may have contracted,
it cannot be worse than the Church which our Saviour found in
Jerusalem : yet he still recommended to the congregation, the duty
of obedience to their spiritual rulers " (*ib.*).   The Government
cannot alter the Church at their pleasure, at least not by right.
' The Church of England never can be altered *legally*, without the
consent and act of the Convocations, who are a part of the Constitution " (IV. 498).   The Holy Communion " can only be offered
by a priest : and all the world cannot make a priest " (IV. 414).

His attitude towards Dissent is instructive.   " It is too much the
fashion of our times to divide the Christian religion into two classes,
one including the Papists, and the other comprehending the

motley herd who are disunited from the Church of Rome, and who
are all distinguished by the general name of Protestants.   Whereas
the Sectarians are many of them as widely removed from us of the
Church of England, as we are from the Papists " (IV. 458). The
typical Dissenter for William Jones is Dr. Priestley, who has recently
threatened us with ruin, that they will " blow up the old rotten fabric
of the Church of England ".   The old persecuting spirit of Puritan-
ism is still there, as the Gordon Riots show (IV. 486–7).   Jones
argues against Socinian tendencies, whether in the Church or in
modern Dissent.   Some of the Dissenters' sermons " approach
nearer to the cold philosophy of Bolingbroke, and the wildness of
Voltaire, than to the faith and language of their forefathers " (V.
221).   All the time there was the suspicion of the Dissenters on
political grounds, as wanting to overthrow the Constitution.[1]

There is little in these volumes about the Methodists, except in
so far as they may be identified with the Enthusiasts.   The general
position is fairly expressed in the *Letter to a Young Gentleman at
Oxford*, where " the particular modes of deceit by which we are
most liable to be infected " are Infidelity (the Deists) ; Enthusiasm
(" the enthusiast . . . delivers himself wholly to divine impulses
and immediate revelations " and gives up outward institutions) ;
Lukewarmness ; and Superstition, which is defined as reliance on
outward forms and attendance at church once a week and occasionally
at Communion, without inner religion.   " If you insist on the absolute necessity of personal holiness, purity of life, and abstraction
from fashionable folly ", you will be called a Methodist (I. 260).

Jones is continually recurring to a favourite thought about the
religious lessons of nature, which is put in an extreme and provoca-
tive form in *The Book of Nature : or, The True Sense of Things,
explained and made easy to the Capacity of Children*.   The book
begins :

> The ass hath. very long ears, and yet he hath no sense of music,
> but brayeth with a fearful noise. . . .
> Q. Which is the child who will not learn ?
> A. An ass, which is ignorant and unruly . . .
> Q. For what end did God make the lark and the dove ?
> A. To teach us what we ought to be.
> Q. Why did he make owls, bats, and swine ?
> A. To teach us what we ought not to be.

[1] Jones refers to the editions of Baxter's *The Saint's Everlasting Rest*
prior to 1660, where for " the Kingdom of Heaven " appeared " the
Parliament of Heaven " (IV. 469).

And this from a leading theologian who was an F.R.S.! Our first impulse is to say, What a silly fellow! But the line of thought has a respectable ancestry. Listen to St. Cyprian (*De Unitate Ecclesiae*, 9):

> The Holy Spirit came in the form of a dove, a guileless and joyous creature, not bitter with gall, not fierce nor apt to bite, not violent nor tearing with its claws; it loves the fellowship of men, dwells in one house; when they breed, they bring up their young ones together; when they fly abroad, they nest close together . . . fulfilling the law of love in all things.
>
> This purity of heart must be recognised in the Church, this affection must be held fast, that brotherly love may imitate doves, that kindliness and gentleness may match those of lambs and sheep. What place in a Christian breast is found for the savagery of wolves, the fierceness of dogs, the deadly poison of snakes, or the fury of wild beasts?

Is not this a legitimate drawing out of the meaning of " Be ye harmless as doves " ?

Jones writes in *Zoologia Ethica* (III. 89): " I think it is but just to assert, that this moral use of the animal creation was originally *intended* in the formation of the world because it would be a supposition unworthy of God, that the works of nature should be capable of answering any good end, which his wisdom did not forsee, and consequently design." And again: " The turpitude of the swine is not moral but natural : it is as blameless as the scent of the dunghill : yet in these things they hold up to us a picture of bad men " (III. 23).

There is a good deal about the dangers of classical education, well expressed but suffering from the error of supposing that the Hebrew language and culture were the primitive ones, from which all others were derived. The theory is supported by many accidental resemblances, such as *shir* (song) = siren, *safar* (write) = cypher. But Jones says that etymology must be used with caution, or " we shall find no mercy from those who are not well affected to the originalities of learning and religion " (XII. 241).

Some interesting sidelights are thrown on the times in the following extracts. " It is hard upon them [the clergy], that in some instances, where the tenths have been surrendered peaceably to laymen, confederacies have been formed and illegal assemblies convened, to prevent the taking of the tenths by clergymen " (V. 308, in 1782). Less than two-thirds of the tithes are collected. In 1789 we are told that funeral sermons are going out of fashion. " The fabulous objects of the Grecian mythology have even got possession of our churches ; in one of which I have seen a monument, with elegant figures as large as the life, of the three Fates, Clotho, Lachesis, and Atropos, spinning and clipping the thread of a great man's life " (III. 430; in Wharton church, near Kettering). A sermon was preached at Pluckley, in Kent, in 1777, when two young women did public penance in church by their own choice—" My desire is to lead you to the proper use which ought to be made of the example we have before us this day in the church " (V. 186). " How happy is the good man in the opportunity of redeeming a poor Christian slave, who has been chained to the oar, and beaten by unfeeling Turkish tyrants " (V. 187). In *Letters from a Tutor to his Pupils* (XI) he says about good manners that " humility, good nature, and good sense " are needed rather than teaching; on temperance— excessive consumption of animal food is harmful, the Church's Calendar (i.e. fast days) is the best physician. As to style—always use a word of native English origin if possible, and take Swift as the standard of English writing. And can we better, as a preacher's judgment, this verdict on the result of the American war ? " A wild spirit of independence prevailed ; and, by the just judgment of God upon a profligate mother, and untutored children, prevailed " (V. 284).

We need not linger over the large part of the Works devoted to Science in its various branches—physics, electricity, meteorology, and sound ; " whether there be knowledge, it shall vanish away ". But we should note his statement that he writes in the style of Seneca and the elder Pliny rather than in the dry manner usually adopted by scientists. His theory of fossils is that the earth's surface was so disturbed by the immense weight of water of the Flood that the fossils were deposited at all depths.

To complete the picture of this many-sided man : Jones was a competent musician and composed services and tunes. In a sermon he urges the use of sixteenth and seventeenth century music. In a treatise *On a Church Organ* he laments that the voluntary is generally " a time for trifling chat ". For nearly every one the memory of this good man has faded away, but very many know his inspiring tune " Nayland " or " St. Stephen ", associated with the baptismal hymn " In token that thou shalt not fear ", the name of which was perhaps suggested by that of his friend William Stevens.

(c) William Stevens

The *Memoirs of William Stevens Esq.* were written by his friend Sir James Alan Park, a judge of the Court of Common Pleas. Published in 1812, the book ran to a second edition in 1814, a third in 1823, a fourth in 1825 ;[1] and was reprinted as late as 1859. The author says that Stevens' Life of William Jones was influenced by the Lives of Isaac Walton ; we may assume that the same is true of the Lives of Bishop Horne and Stevens. All three books are marked by unusual lightness of touch.

Stevens was born in Southwark on March 2nd, 1732. His father, who was a tradesman, died when he and his sister were infants. Their mother went to live near her brother Samuel Horne, the Rector of Otham, near Maidstone, and so William Stevens was brought up with his cousin, the future Bishop Horne, whose school-fellow he was. He left school at fourteen and was apprenticed to a Mr. Hookham, wholesale hosier, of 68 Old Broad Street, at which house he lived continuously until his death. In 1754 Mr. Hookham made him a partner. When he died, Stevens became chief partner, which he remained until 1801, when he retired from active participation in the business, but continued to board with his successor. In 1807 he died suddenly and was buried in the churchyard of Otham, where a monument to him was erected in the church. He never married.

" Mr. Stevens spent all his leisure time " in study. He " acquired . . . not only an intimate acquaintance with the French language, but also attained to a considerable knowledge of Latin, Greek, and Hebrew literature : and became one of the profoundest theologians of his time ". At the age of seventeen he engaged a French master, who attended three days a week for an hour at a time ; in a year he had mastered the language. As a Hutchinsonian he was naturally drawn to the study of Hebrew ; Parkhurst, compiler of Greek and Hebrew Lexicons, dedicated the latter to four persons, described as " the favourers and promoters " of the work, one of whom was Stevens. He was well read in the early Fathers, and in the Anglican Divines, especially Andrewes, Jeremy Taylor and Hickes. He read a great deal of history and, moving much in literary society, kept up with contemporary literature. The Bishop of Salisbury (Dr. Douglas) in a company of Bishops, when Stevens was present,

[1] The fourth edition has been used.

said : " Here is a man, who, though not a Bishop, yet would have been thought worthy of that character in the first and purest ages of the Christian Church." [1]

His literary output, which was not large, was collected in a volume entitled Ουδενος εργα (*The Works of Nobody*). " Nobody " became the name by which his friends knew him, and in 1800 a club called " Nobody's " was founded in his honour. It lasted for a long time ; indeed, the statement found in Overton and Relton's *History* (1906), " His memory is perpetuated by the well known Church Club, called ' Nobody's ' or ' The Club of Nobody's Friends ' ", shows that it lasted into the twentieth century. I am told that it still exists.

The earliest of his works, like the rest no more than a pamphlet, except for the Life of William Jones, was published anonymously in 1773 : *An Essay on the Nature and Constitution of the Christian Church.* (The S.P.C.K. published an edition as late as 1837.) The Church is not a voluntary society, but a spiritual one founded by Christ in opposition to the kingdom of darkness. In the New Testament it has three orders—Apostles, priests and deacons. The Church today draws its commission from God. The Bishops, who succeeded the Apostles, have " the plenitude of power " ; " the priests and deacons [have it] by an authority derived from them ". The power includes law-making, jurisdiction, and exclusion from the community.

In 1776 Stevens measured swords with Dr. Richard Watson, afterwards Bishop of Llandaff, who had published two sermons preached before the University of Cambridge, answering them by two pamphlets, of which a letter written in that year said : " The Divinity-Professor's low-flying sermon has received strictures from a wealthy hosier. . . . He is a Tory of the old *Filmer* stamp, and will not convince, or please many readers ; yet he is not without some good strokes at the Doctor. But *non tali auxilio*—the Whigs are the most affected by such rhapsodies." [2]

His Churchmanship was shown by constant attendance at Sunday services,[3] morning and afternoon ; by never missing an opportunity

[1] In the latter part of his life Stevens was auditor of the S.P.G. and Treasurer of Queen Anne's Bounty, and was personally known to all the Bishops.

[2] J. Nichols, *Illustrations of the Literary History of the Eighteenth Century,* I. 160. Sir Robert Filmer was a seventeenth century writer severely attacked by Locke.

[3] So punctilious was he that he would always " stand when the praises of God were sung, even though in a congregation, where he might be the solitary instance of this decorous and becoming usage ".

of receiving Holy Communion ; and by daily churchgoing.   Alluding to the falling off in this last observance, " this cheerful man, who had his joke always ready, having observed his own banker one day in church, at weekly prayers, as they walked out when the service was over, in his lively manner said to him, ' if you will not tell of me, I will not tell of you ' ".   (The biographer assumes that the daily offices were said in some City churches at least.)   Living alone and as a boarder he could not practise family prayer.   " In his private devotions Mr. Stevens was regular and constant ; and wherever he went in the country, he carried with him his Hebrew Bible and Greek Testament—and uniformly read the lessons for the day, before he left his chamber, in their original languages."

The only details given of his appearance are that he " dressed like a clergyman, in black clothes, and a bushy clerical wig ", and an extract from his diary : " turned myself out of bed soon after six o'clock—shaved my head all over—an easier task than formerly—thanks to Old Time ".   He was particularly fond of young people, who were much attracted by him.   " Playfulness and humour were to the last his prominent qualities : he was a great laugher at any neat or smart observation, and would stamp his feet in the exuberance of his mirth : he had no objection to a quiet rubber at whist, but rather enjoyed it ; and, in short, even to the last week of his life, he did not think it unbecoming his character to mix in all the innocent cheerfulness of domestic life."   But among strangers he was shy and reserved ; he felt his loneliness in being " neither father, husband, uncle, brother ",[1] and in a private paper noted that the reserve which he ascribed to humility was probably the effect of pride.

The story of the Scottish Episcopal Church need not be told here.   Until the consecration of Bishop Seabury, Stevens did not know of its existence.   But when three Bishops (Skinner, Drummond and Strachan) came to London in 1789 to arrange for the removal of the penal statutes,[2] he met them and with the Rev. Dr. Gaskin (Secretary of the S.P.C.K.) and Mr. J. A. Park (writer of his Life)

[1] His sister must have died without issue.

[2] In justice to the Government it should be remembered that there was a *prima facie* case for suspecting the loyalty of the Episcopalians.   " The heads of this Church, upon the death of the only person who continued his claim; in opposition to the reigning family, in April 1788, found themselves at liberty to call upon the clergy and laity, over whom they were placed, to acknowledge their attachment to the present government of the kingdom, as vested in his Majesty King George the Third ; and to direct that public prayers for the King *by name* should be authoritatively introduced, and afterwards continued in the religious assemblies of that Church " (Park, *Memoirs*, pp. 92–3).

became a " Committee for managing in England the Affairs of the Scottish Episcopal Church ". Their efforts were crowned with success in 1792. The controversy enabled Stevens to clear his mind on questions of Churchmanship ; in a letter to Bishop Skinner (May 1st, 1797) he formulated his views in a sentence well in advance of public opinion : " Making establishment necessary to the existence of the Church, as many are apt to do, is a grievous mistake ; but to be sure it is a convenient appendage ; and there is no harm in kings being nursing fathers, if they will nurse it properly."

Another quotation from a letter will show the admirable good sense and style of William Stevens ; also that Dr. Johnson's manner of speaking was shared by others. He recommends " the associating the old with the young ; and it may be profitable to both, as with a little attention it may serve to keep all parties in good humour, which is a very good thing ; it may make the old, by the lively, agreeable conversation of the young, forget their infirmities ; and it may lead the young, from observing the calmed passions and placid manners of the old, to consider old age, to which they are advancing, as no uncomfortable state, nor any formidable evil ".

Lastly we must consider the way Stevens practised almsgiving. He was a member of the S.P.G. and the S.P.C.K., a governor of many hospitals, a subscriber of over £50 a year to the Clergy Orphan School, and a liberal benefactor in cases of distress among the clergy made known to him through Queen Anne's Bounty. He paid a tenth part of his income to a special fund entitled *Clericus*, and another tenth to a similar fund *Pauper*. He kept careful accounts of these funds, considering himself a trustee and allowing interest on the unspent balance. He found himself unable to keep these funds solvent and had to come to the rescue with further gifts to wipe out large deficits. A further item was entitled *Gifts*, to cover contributions which, though desirable, were not strictly charity, such as the education of poor lads at the University. Considerably more than half his income, which in a typical year was £1200, was spent in these three ways. He would never give his name to a fashionable public subscription, where no doubt existed that the money required would be forthcoming. He parted with large capital sums as well as income, by purchasing annuities for destitute people. Applications for assistance were more than his lavish generosity could cope with, so he founded a small body called " The Berean Society ", which undertook work like educating ordinands at Oxford.[1] Asked

---

[1] Perhaps the Society was a periphrasis for himself.

in 1800 to be a steward at the annual dinner of the Bridewell and Bethlehem Hospitals he replied : " Mr. Stevens . . . is very ready to accept of the appointment to be steward this year ; but submits it to the consideration of the governors and the gentlemen in rotation, whether in these times of scarcity, it is not more advisable for the rich to fast, that the poor may not starve." The suggestion was accepted, the dinner was abandoned, and the cost of it (£300) given to the poor. In the characterization of himself already mentioned he says : " A melancholy cast, sometimes, leads him to the habitations of the afflicted ; and being too indolent to withhold his money, he suffers it to be taken from him on the slightest pretence, mistaking it is to be feared, vice for virtue, self-indulgence for charity." Stevens had little to learn either from the Christian stewardship of riches practised by the Clapham Evangelicals or from the investigations of modern psychologists into motives.

One gift deserves to be recorded as a fitting conclusion to this sketch, a private communion set sent to a priest, bearing texts— inside the paten " He was known of them in breaking of bread ", outside " Behold the Lamb of God " ; on the chalice " When I see the blood I will pass over you ", and on its foot " For Christ is our peace ".

Since the first edition of this book was published, by the kindness of Mr. Clifton Kelway, I have been told about the Club of " Nobody's Friends."

Founded in 1800 it has met three times a year until the present day except during the two world-wars. The membership, which for a long time has been restricted to fifty, has included many famous names : at least eighty-seven Bishops and fifty Judges, Earl Balfour, Lord Esher, Viscount Halifax, etc. The family of Gibbs (Lord Aldenham) has been represented for more than a hundred years. Thirty extra members (Bishops and Judges) are allowed. Each new member is " challenged " and has to " justify " himself by pronouncing an " éloge " on himself.

X

GOOD MRS. TRIMMER

Mrs. Trimmer was once a household name. The children of the well to do were brought up on *The History of the Robins*; the poor on her school books. She appears in Byron's *Don Juan*,[1] and as "good Mrs. Trimmer" as late as C. S. Calverley.[2] To those living today who have heard her name it suggests a very old-fashioned and almost absurd lady. The reality is quite different, nothing less than a heroine and saint.

Some Account of the Life and Writings of Mrs. Trimmer (2 volumes, 1814) is a work which cannot be read without emotion. It consists in the main of extracts from her private Journal, kept during twenty-five years, in which she pours forth her soul in prayer. The contrast between the lucid, concise style of her books written for publication, with their mass of facts, and the monotonous, artless repetitions of the Journal is so marked that no thought of its publication can have crossed her mind.

Sarah Kirby (her maiden name) was born at Ipswich in 1741, her father Joshua being a teacher of art and a writer of repute in his day; the home was deeply religious. She went to an Ipswich boarding school, where she learned French thoroughly. When she was fourteen the family moved to London, her father having been appointed art teacher to the Prince of Wales, afterwards George III. She moved in literary and artistic circles, and Dr. Johnson, Gainsborough, Hogarth, etc. were among her friends. Johnson was much struck by her when, at a gathering at Sir Joshua Reynolds' house, the talk turned on *Paradise Lost* and she produced a copy from her pocket. "He invited her the next day to his house, presented her with a copy of his Rambler, and afterwards treated her with great consideration" (*Life*, I. 9). She spent much of her time

---

[1] In short, she was a walking calculator,
    Miss Edgeworth's novels stepping from their covers,
Or Mrs. Trimmer's books on education,
    Or "Coelebs' wife" set out in search of lovers. (I. xvi.)

[2] *Fly Leaves* (1866): "Lovers, and a Reflection" (Of song birds).
    They need no parasols, no goloshes;
    And good Mrs. Trimmer she feedeth them—
suggested presumably by *The Robins*.

in reading and drawing, and used to help her only brother (she had
no sister), who was at Westminster School, with his home work.

In 1759 her father went to live at Kew, where he had been appointed
clerk of the works at the Palace. Here she met Mr. Trimmer,
who was two years older than herself, marrying him at the age of
twenty-one, and setting up house at Brentford. Six boys and six
girls were born of the marriage; nine of the children were alive
when she died. Years of unremitting toil were her lot. She
undertook the entire education of the family herself, except for the
boys' classics, taught by a neighbouring clergyman, and devised a
system by which the elder children instructed the younger. In the
evenings, when Mr. Trimmer returned from business, he would
read aloud to the family—Shakespeare, Milton, Pope, Addison,
and the works of standard divines. Even at this period she visited
the poor constantly, especially in sickness. Her physique must
have been remarkable, for she sat up after the rest of the family
had gone to bed, and rose at five, sometimes at four, even in severe
winter weather, to get through her work at busy periods. The habit
was formed before marriage, when she got up very early to learn
poetry. She and a friend living on the opposite bank of the river
use to vie with each other in early rising, hanging up white hand-
kerchiefs in the bedroom windows as a sign that they were up.

Her career as an author began in 1780, when she began to put her
instructions of the children into book form. The first volume
of the *Sacred History* appeared in 1782, the work being eventually
completed in six volumes. *Fabulous Histories*, afterwards called
The History of the Robins, followed shortly afterwards. The
Prayer Book and the Bible were explained in a number of books;
A Help to the Unlearned commented on every chapter of the Bible.
Her moral tales and school readers had a large circulation. Anticipating Charlotte Yonge's *Monthly Packet*, she was the sole author as
well as editor of *The Family Magazine*, each number of which contained a sermon abridged from an Anglican divine, descriptions
of foreign countries (pointing out how much worse off the poor were
than in England), and instructive tales. *The Oeconomy of Charity*
(1786) dealt with the problems of Sunday Schools and, with her other
books, helped to prepare the way for the foundation of the National
Society. It was her conviction that the Charity Schools had become
stereotyped in their methods and confined to a comparatively few
children, so that new methods were required. The wonderful
old lady, whose simplicity, modesty, intellectual ability and gentle-

ness, shine out in the biography and still more in the Journal, died in
her chair in 1810.

The Journal has many entries describing the joy of Holy Communion. "Blessed Jesus, I am this day going to renew my baptismal vow at thy holy table" (Feb. 12th, 1786). "I received
the Sacrament on Christmas Day, but not with that fervour of
devotion which I hoped to feel. The next day I received it with a
sick person, and since then at church again" (Jan. 14th, 1791).[1]
In 1793 : "The Lord's supper . . . is a means, and a most blessed
one, of repairing the breaches of a former covenant . . . everyone
has repeatedly broken the covenant into which he entered by the
Sacrament of Baptism, and cannot be restored to its privileges without having recourse to the other Sacrament for the renewal of them."
In the same year : "If my life be spared I will try to bring the poor
to the Sacrament."

It was her practice to retire for two or three hours on Sunday
evening to be alone with her Journal. There are many confessions
of failure to write it up owing to the increasing demands of the
Sunday Schools. She was a friend and correspondent of Robert
Raikes and Hannah More, and a pioneer of the movement in the
London districts. In Hannah More's Letters, published in 1834,
we have two charming references to her friend. January 1788, to
her sister : "I carried good Mrs. Trimmer there [the Bishop of
Salisbury's—Shute Barrington] yesterday. The Bishop diverted
us by saying he was between two very singular women, one who
undertook to reform all the *poor*, and the other all the *great* ; but he
congratulated her on having the most hopeful subjects." [2] And
May 1788, also to her sister : "Among my country excursions I
must not omit dining with Mrs. Trimmer and her twelve children
at Brentford—a scene too of instruction and delight." In November
1786 Mrs. Trimmer went to see the Queen to advise on the starting
of Sunday Schools at Windsor, and letters arrived from all over the
country asking for advice. "Thanksgivings a thousand times
repeated, could not express the transports of my heart, which over-
flows with joy and gratitude when I reflect on the success of the
Sunday Schools" (1786). The organization was a heavy responsibility. In many places the children had to be clothed by the efforts
of charitable ladies. Mrs. Trimmer's practice was to allow the

---

[1] Contrast the popular idea of Communion four times a year at this
period.
[2] Miss More's *Thoughts on the Importance of the Manners of the Great*
had just been published, making a furore.

parents 2d. in the 1/- for the cost of clothing.[1] The Master, who was generally paid, was assisted by voluntary teachers. Mrs. Trimmer showed great interest in a spinning-wheel, to be bought for £5, by which eighteen children could spin at once. The Sunday School taught reading and handwork, besides religious knowledge, and with attendance at church took up most of the children's Sunday. In 1792 she refers to the great pecuniary loss caused her by the Schools. A little later she seems to have had other losses, for she writes that the loss of property is to be met " by an increase of charity in every duty of religion, particularly in charity to the poor as far as my ability extends " (II. 72).

Mr. Trimmer died in 1792 and for the rest of her life was mourned, but with a complete absence of the morbidity then fashionable, at least among Evangelicals. In 1796 the widow revisited her birthplace at Ipswich and with special joy saw the font where she had been baptized. By this time she could write : " My family which receives the addition of three or four grandchildren every year, calls my attention in various ways." After her husband's death she seems to have moved to Ealing, where the task of starting Sunday Schools began over again. The Journal reveals her entering acutely into the joys and sorrows of her children, caring for the spiritual welfare of her maids, agonizing over lapsed Sunday School children, and, as if this were not enough, taking on other burdens. Thus she had to support a girl, the daughter of affluent parents, who had cast her off because of a marriage with a man of the working class, and with whom she pleaded in vain for reconciliation. The poor young woman, whose husband was out of work, eventually died, with her baby, as a result of privations. " How fatal are the consequences of disobedience ! how destructive the unrelenting severity of offended parents ! " wrote Mrs. Trimmer in her Journal (II. 142).

With all her burdens, the note of joy predominated. The beauty of nature, pointing to the goodness of its Creator, was a continual source of thankfulness. Her humility and deference to Church authority are illustrated by an entry of Feb. 5th, 1793. " This is the day that is to determine the success of the plan I have formed for the improvement of the education of the poor ; desirous as I am that it

---

[1] When I went to be Rector of a Suffolk village in 1908 the Sunday School children used to pay 1d. a week, sometimes more, and receive their contributions at the end of the year plus 2d. in the 1s., in the form of a ticket on a shop, which allowed a further 2d. in the 1s. This may have gone back to Mrs. Trimmer's original impulse.

I

should be adopted by the Society for Promoting Christian Knowledge, I feel at present very calm and easy about it, and I hope I
shall continue to do so ; the honour of my Saviour, and the good of
the poor, are the sole ends I have in view."   The decision was
delayed, and not till June 19th did she record that the S.P.C.K. had
adopted her books for Charity Schools.

A description of all her books is outside the scope of this sketch ;
but something needs to be said to complete the picture. *The
Charity School Spelling Book* Part I contains " The Alphabet,
Spelling Lessons, and Short Stories of Good and Bad Boys, in
words of one syllable only ". (A similar book for girls is identical,
except that the stories are of Good and Bad Girls.) The lessons
are masterly in the skill with which they keep to words of one syllable.
Some of the sentences illustrate the children's life. " The Girl
spins fine yarn. The Boy heads pins well. The Boy mends
his own coat. The Girl makes the boy's shirt. Good Girls make
their own clothes. Good Boys take care of their shoes." " When
you sit [in church] you should sit straight upon the form, and not
put your feet out to kick or throw people down. When Psalms
are sung you should stand up, and not sit all the while, as some
people do."

Here is one extract from the stories. A man says to a poor boy
in the street : " I know of a school where they will not mind your
rags, where you may learn to read, and to put heads on pins, and
help to make shoes and boots, and mend your clothes." The
Second Part contains over 100 pages and has explanations of the hard
words of the Bible. In another Lesson Book the Prayer Book is
taught with extraordinary detail and accuracy.

Instructive Tales for adults grew out of her work for children.
She wanted to help those who had left school and so wrote these
artless stories of good and bad people in humble spheres of life.
The " good poor " are no doubt based on favourable examples of the
thousands with whom she came into contact, though presumably
she idealized her favourites, as all generous-hearted people are apt
to do. Observing this caution we can use the tales as background
material for the social history of the time.

The Servant's Friend was written partly " to direct the young
and inexperienced in the proper choice of masters and mistresses ",
partly to inculcate faithful service. " The connexion between
masters and mistresses and servants is of a very endearing nature."

Servants should be "humble friends"—"humble" was an in-
evitable epithet at a time when subordination was so much empha-
sized, "friends" was a new note.

Thomas, a village boy, in this tale goes to a Charity School at
eleven, clad in "the coat of grey, the band and cap, and other articles
which composed the uniform of the school". We need only notice a
scene where two of his schoolfellows are caught stealing apples.
The owners take them off to "the cage, where they sat, exposed to
the derision of all the village, without a morsel of food". In the
evening "the boys were taken out by the constable, who, tying their
arms to their backs, fastened a rope to each, and drove them before
him, while a crowd of men, women, and children, surrounded them,
hooting and reproaching all the way". The justice dismissed them
with a caution. After leaving school Thomas is taken on as Rector's
boy at a salary of £4 a year. The various maidservants whom
he meets provide a text for advice about their duties and opportunities.

The Two Farmers is called "An Exemplary Tale; designed to
recommend the practice of benevolence towards mankind, and all
other living creatures; and the religious observance of the Sabbath-
day". Mrs. Trimmer seems to have been a pioneer in the campaign
against cruelty to animals, which looms large in her school books
as well as in the tales. In this book, as elsewhere, indecent ballads
are condemned; but a model peasant woman sings certain un-
objectionable ones as she spins—The Berkshire Lady, Fair Rosa-
mond, The Lamentations of Jane Shore, and Chevy Chace. An
interesting description is given of a small farmer's house, consisting
of kitchen, parlour, and four bedrooms.

"In the kitchen was an open chimney, which admitted of two
forms, one on each side; on these the men and boys sat very com-
fortably of a winter's evening, and ate their bread and cheese, while
they listened to the conversation which passed at an open table,
round which were usually placed the farmer, his wife, and mother.
. . . The chairs were of deal, with rush bottoms, and one of them
had elbows to it; this was intended for the master of the house,
that he might be distinguished from his domestics."

The prints on the walls are enumerated. "The first of them
was a print representing our Saviour's humility, and the pope's
pride; over this he hung the Golden Rule, and the summary of
the law and the prophets. On one side of it was a very droll print
called the Happy Marriage; and on the other, a dialogue called
Death and the Lady, with the print to it. There was another print

entitled Keep within Compass ; and one representing a miser raking gold together, and a spendthrift throwing it about. Mr. Simpkins had also bought, to paste up among them, *The Way to Wealth*, taken from *Poor Richard's Almanack*.[1] So much for the kitchen. The parlour sounds enchanting, but the description is too long to quote.

At Christmas time the holidays seem to last for a week or two. The men and boys, who " live in ", are allowed to go home to their respective villages in turn, for a day or two each.

In the other tales different types of character and employment are described. The most interesting are *The Good Schoolmistress* and *The Good Nurse*.

Mrs. Fairfield, the schoolmistress, was in good service ; when she was nearly thirty her mistress died, leaving her a small legacy. She then married an exciseman and had a family of two girls. Anxious to supplement her husband's earnings, she opened a school, first reading, " with great attention, a valuable book, written by Dr. Talbot . . . entitled The Christian Schoolmaster, from which she formed her plan of proceedings ". (Mrs. Trimmer earnestly recommends this book to all who keep Charity or Sunday Schools.) The scholars were few in number, for few could afford to pay the fees. Soon afterwards her husband died. The new Rector then started a Sunday School, having raised a subscription for the purpose of providing the stipend. Mrs. Fairfield was appointed school-mistress, the girls being limited to thirty ; and a master was found for the same number of boys. The work was less than on weekdays, because of the help given by ladies, who were so much interested that they clubbed together and raised the money with which to pay the fees (4*d*. a week) of the poorer children, to enable them to go to the weekday school also. So popular was Mrs. Fairfield that some of the parents voluntarily paid 6*d*. a week. The girls learned to make and mend all their clothing, and to cut out nearly all. She would not, like most mistresses, resort to corporal punishment.

The advice given in *The Good Nurse* is by no means out of date so far as behaviour goes ; Mrs. Trimmer deals admirably with such points as getting on with the servants, and what to do when you find bad practices going on in the kitchen, which must generally be tolerated, because mentioning them to the mother of a new-born baby would worry her and do no good. Appended to the story

[1] Compare the description of the prints on the walls of a cottage in Crabbe, *The Parish Register*, Part I. See p. 129.

are her own rules for the management of children. Over-feeding
of infants is a great evil; so is excess of clothing. The baby should
be accustomed to the open air from at least a fortnight old and
be given exercise from the first. Rocking should be avoided.
Meat must not be given to a child until he has teeth with which to
chew—this is nature's message. A young child must not be sent
to school unless the mistress will let him spend a good part of the
time in the open air. Not all the advice is in accordance with modern
ideas, but the nurses trained on Mrs. Trimmer lines were far from
being Mrs. Gamps.

The presupposition of all Mrs. Trimmer's tales is the inevitability
and rightness of class distinctions. It would be a quite unhistorical
judgment to find fault with her for this. She wrote for the world as
she knew it, a world in which there were multitudes of poor people
living in squalor and ignorance, and in bad times in danger of starvation. At the other extreme there were the rich, largely profligate
in their habits and unmindful of social responsibilities. The State
did nothing for the education of the poor; it remained for the
religious middle class to step into the breach and help them to be
clean, moral, self-respecting, God-fearing. Right nobly they did
their duty. There is no trace in Mrs. Trimmer's writings of fear
that in default of their efforts revolutionary outbreaks might occur
which would sweep her and her class away. As her stories show,
education did in favourable cases provide a ladder which might
lead from the working class to the middle class. In the nineteenth
century the habits of self-help and austere frugality learned in the
hard school of the Napoleonic wars produced a virile and versatile
nation able to take advantage of the opportunities of world-wide
expansion. The social conscience then almost confined to Christians
of the type of Mrs. Trimmer and expressed in their heroic activities
is now shown in the institutions of the State. The greatness of
Victorian England, which grew out of an extreme of social insecurity,
is an established fact of history. If social security can be won the
gain will be immense: what the corresponding loss will be, in
freedom and individuality, will be for the historian of the future to
assess. He may even judge that people like Mrs. Trimmer were as
great in their generation as are the famous social reformers of our
day in theirs.

XI

THE CHURCH IN CRABBE'S POEMS

GEORGE CRABBE'S poems are so familiar that a discussion of them here might seem unnecessary. But since these essays in the main tend to emphasize the better side of Church life in the eighteenth century, something is needed to redress the balance, and nothing can do this better than his poems.

Crabbe's early struggles are pitiful to read about; he knew from bitter experience the realities he described. One of his purposes was to prick the bubble of the fashionable idealizing of rural felicity. This he did with a success which was a credit to the literary taste of his time—within his limits Crabbe's skill in the use of rhymed couplets is amazing. In his later life the tide had turned; romance had come in again and his vogue passed.

The fabric of the churches was suffering from the hand of time :

> Meanwhile the building slowly falls away
> And, like the builders, will in time decay.
>
> *The Borough*, II.

Monuments are mangled as if by war. Our indignation at the misguided zeal of nineteenth century church restorers is tempered when we remember that when a further fifty years had passed the fabrics were in such a state that rebuilding was often the only course open. Gothic was no longer a term of abuse.

> " You noble Gothic arch ", " That Gothic door "
> So have they said; of proof you'll need no more.
>
> *Ib.*

The eighteenth century craze for mural tablets is satirized.

> But we have mural tablets, every size,
> That woe could wish, or vanity devise.
>
> *Ib.*

The duet of parson and clerk is perfectly summarized in four lines.

> Where priest and clerk with joint exertion strive
> To keep the ardour of their flock alive;
> That, by his periods eloquent and grave;
> This, by responses, and a well set stave.
>
> *Ib.*

The Ante-Communion Service has become so divorced from the Service proper that

> Not at the altar our young brethren read
> (Facing their flock) the Decalogue and Creed;
> But at their duty, in their desks they stand,
> With naked surplice, lacking hood and band.
>
> *Ib.*, III.

Celebrations are monthly.

> Once in a month the sacramental bread
> Our clerk with wine upon the table spread.[1]
>
> *Ib.*, XIX.

The Vicar bewails the changes.

> Churches are now of holy song bereft
> And half our ancient customs changed or left;
> Few sprigs of ivy are at Christmas seen,
> Nor crimson berry tips the holly's green;
> Mistaken choirs refuse the solemn strain
> Of ancient Sternhold, which from ours amain
> Comes flying forth from aisle to aisle about
> Sweet links of harmony and well drawn out.
>
> *Ib.*, III.

A sad story is told of dishonesty. The parish clerk took round the alms box at the end of a long wand[2]—

> Tall, spacious seats the wealthier people hid,
> And none had view of what his neighbour did.
>
> *Ib.*, XIX.

His dishonesty was not detected until a year had passed, and then by means of marked coins, after the widows had complained that their doles had decreased.[3]

Crabbe apologizes " for the insertion of a circumstance by no means common " when he describes the funeral of a pauper in the absence of the clergyman.

> The busy priest detained by weightier care,
> Defers his duty till the day of prayer;
> And, waiting long, the crowd retire distress'd
> To think a poor man's bones should lie unbless'd.
>
> *The Village*, I.

[1] Not on a credence table.

[2] The wand was necessary to reach distant pews. I remember the method's being used in unrestored churches when I was a boy.

[3] A new Rector coming to a Suffolk village in 1895 was confronted, in the week following the first Communion Sunday, by the widows, demanding *their* money, which had been withheld. His predecessor had divided the alms among the widows who had communicated.

Evidently the poor are buried without coffins.

> Their graves soon levell'd to the earth, and then
> Will other hillocks rise o'er other men;
> Daily the dead on the decay'd are thrust,
> And generations follow, " dust to dust ".

The Borough, II.

But in the chancel "sleep the departed vicars of the place" (*Ib.*, III).
Sermons are described as judged by the Methodists.

> They give their moral precepts; so, they say,
> Did Epictetus once, and Seneca . . .
> Hark to the churchman: day by day he cries
> " Children of men, be virtuous and wise;
> Seek patience, justice, temperance, meekness, truth;
> In age be courteous, be sedate in youth ! "—
> So they advise, and when such things be read,
> How can we wonder that their flocks are dead ? . . .
> And lo ! with all their learning, when they rise
> To preach, in view the ready sermon lies;
> Some low-prized stuff they purchased at the stalls,
> And more like Seneca's than mine or Paul's.

Ib., IV.

Needless to say, Crabbe does not endorse this verdict. "I have
nothing to observe of the Calvinist and Arminian, considered as
such; but my remarks are pointed at the enthusiast and the bigot,
at their folly and their craft" (Preface to *The Borough*).

The Vicar is a gentle, idle man, diligent in visiting the small gentry.

> No haughty virtues stirr'd his peaceful mind,
> Nor urg'd the priest to leave his flock behind . . .
> His frequent visits never failed to please;
> Easy himself, he sought his neighbour's ease.

Ib., III.

But he craves even greater peace.

> That ease be mine, which after all his cares,
> The pious, peaceful prebendary shares . . .
> Now rests our vicar.   They who knew him best,
> Proclaim his life to have been entirely rest,
> Nor one so old has left this world of sin,
> More like the being that he entered in.

Ib.

The curate is a pitiable object.

> Behold his dwelling, this poor hut he hires,
> Where he from view, though not from want retires;
> Where four fair daughters, and five sorrowing sons,
> Partake his sufferings, and dismiss his duns.

Ib.

Of death-bed scenes we read :

> I've seldom known, though I have often read,
> Of happy peasants on their dying bed . . .
> His merits thus and not his hopes confess'd,
> He speaks his hopes, and leaves to Heaven the rest.
> *The Parish Register*, III.

The poor are largely illiterate.

> Much have I tried to guide the fist along,
> But still the blunderers placed their blotting wrong :
> Behold these marks uncouth ! how strange that men
> Who guide the plough, should fail to guide the pen.
> *Ib.*, II.

But there are schools of sorts.

> To every class we have a school assign'd
> Rules for all ranks and food for every mind.
> *The Borough*, XXIV.

In view of Crabbe's early struggles and the poverty from which he emerged it is surprising to find him viewing the poor in so detached a way. " The Poor are here almost of necessity introduced, for they must be considered, in every place, as a large and interesting portion of its inhabitants. I am aware of the great difficulty of acquiring just notions on the maintenance and management of this class of our fellow-subjects " (Preface to *The Borough*). However, he describes a cot of " th' industrious swain " to the best of his ability. The pictures on the wall include The Last Louis in Prison, Charles I and his Golden Rules, Charles II, Lady Godiva, The stoutest Ox in England, a prize fighter, and The Battle of the Nile. A shelf of books contains *The Pilgrim's Progress*, romances bought from the peddler, *The Wandering Jew, Tom Thumb, Jack the Giant-killer*.

> These are the peasant's joy, when placed at ease,
> Half his delighted offspring mount his knees . . .
> There pious works for Sunday's use are found,
> Companions for that Bible newly bound :
> That Bible, bought by sixpence weekly sav'd,
> Has choicest prints by famous hands engrav'd.
> *The Parish Register*, I.

It is depressing to find what a large part is played by seduction, resulting in illegitimate children (*The Parish Register* II), but pleasant to read of the many clubs—for card-players, freemasons, or smokers, a " free-and-easy ", and the poor man's benefit club.

> The printed rules he guards with painted frame,
> And shows his children where to read his name.
>
> *The Borough*, X.

There is enough drabness in Crabbe to satisfy the most pessimistic judgment of the eighteenth century Church.   However, the criticism of doctors and lawyers is equally severe.

XII

A PARISH PRIEST IN THE EIGHTEEN-THIRTIES

A BRIEF account of a forgotten book, describing a faithful priest whose ministry saw its beginnings before 1833, the beginning of the Tractarian Movement, may be welcomed by some readers. The book is called *Practical Religion Exemplified by Letters and Passages from the Life of the late Rev. Robert Anderson, Perpetual Curate of Trinity Chapel, Brighton*; the author was his wife, the Hon. Mrs. Anderson. It was published by Rivingtons, apparently for the S.P.C.K., whose book-list is bound up with my copy (sixth edition, 1855).

Anderson was ordained in 1821 by the Bishop of London, having been Assistant Professor of Oriental Languages at the East India College, Haileybury. In 1825 he became Proprietor and Perpetual Curate of Trinity Chapel, which, formerly a Dissenting Chapel, was consecrated in 1826. He and his wife were well-to-do people. They had a butler and a number of servants, who could not have been maintained on the salary of the minister. (In 1847, when F. W. Robertson went there, the income was £300 and the congregation consisted mainly of tradesmen and servants.) He stayed there till his death in 1843.

We are struck by his intense piety. Even as a boy, " when he returned from school, instead of the foolish presents generally made by boys, he brought his sisters Young's *Night Thoughts* and Milton's *Paradise Lost* " (p. 152). At Brighton " he always rose at six o'clock, that he might contemplate the rising sun, which faced his window; and feeling his heart warmed by the Sun of Righteousness, prostrated himself, like Daniel of old, in humility before his God and Saviour " (p. 156). To his five children he was a loving father, pouring out his soul in long letters to them whenever he was absent; the subjects of the letters were generally details of biblical exegesis and explanations of the Catechism. A sentence from a letter of 1841 illustrates the difference between then and now. " You have often heard me speak of the good Archbishop Leighton; and his observations on this point are so admirable, that I shall here repeat them to you . . ." (p. 131). The most devout of clerical fathers today would shrink from such conversation, for fear of boring his children and setting them against the Church. Family prayers

were held at 9 a.m. and 10 p.m.   Afraid of wearying his household,
he seldom exceeded a quarter of an hour on each occasion.   So orderly
was he that he could lay his hand on any book or paper in the dark,
so friendly that he invariably left his study door open to invite visitors.
Never until his last illness did he fail to dress for dinner.   His
favourite authors were George Herbert, Jeremy Taylor, Donne,
John Smith, and above all Keble, whose *Christian Year* was published
in 1827.

The unconscious class-feeling of the age is betrayed in his remark
about servants : " Our relation to those beneath us is meant as a faint
emblem of the relation in which God has seen good to place himself
with regard to us " ;   also children " should be taught to feel that they
cannot do without servants " (p. 51).   His care for the souls of the
servants is illustrated thus : " It was his custom on Sunday morning
to give them each a tract, which he took the greatest pains to select,
carefully avoiding all unsound and exciting doctrine " (p. 173).

Now here it would seem is a typical Evangelical, in spite of the
unusual choice of favourite authors.   But such a judgment is not
borne out by what follows.   In an undated extract from his diary,
but in any case prior to 1832, we read that " Mr. S. described the
change in his mind since his attendance at Trinity Chapel, from
Latitudinarianism to Catholicism " (p. 159).   When he first went
to Brighton he was considered Low Church.   He was accused of
having become a High Churchman as a result of the Tracts.   However, he was able to prove that his views on doctrinal points had
undergone no change by referring to a sermon of 1826 and to a
pastoral letter of 1832 which told the congregation how he had fulfilled
the pledges of 1826.   As the Tracts began to be published in 1833,
they had no bearing on the point (p. 199).

Anderson seems to have said the daily offices at home (p. 37).
We read of " frequent communions, both on week-days and on
Sundays ", a service every Wednesday, and a Sunday School teachers'
instruction once a month, " reading them passages from the most
approved divines, Leighton, Hooker, and others of the same kind,
and closing with an exposition of Scripture and a Prayer " (p. 222).
Sermons were composed with great care, the writing of them being
spread over four days, Monday to Friday ;   after a while the manuscript was left behind (p. 232).

Writing to his brother, he recommends weekly Communion
if the opportunity is given at the church he attends.   For himself
he says, " It might occasionally happen that my bodily frame would

really be unequal to three hours' intense devotion ". To obviate this difficulty, he longs for the institution of early celebrations (pp. 200–1).

To show his pastoral zeal, we are told that as many as thirty callers would come in a morning ; visits up to fifteen were paid in the afternoon ; and he went out freely in the evening, presumably to the better-off members of the congregation, always however returning for family prayers at 10 p.m.

Lastly I must transcribe a passage on Confirmation, which is strikingly different from the usual account of pre-Tractarian ways (p. 211).

The mention of our Bishop [Otter, 1836–1840] brings me to the subject of the Confirmation which took place yesterday at St. Peter's church. Though only two years have elapsed since our last Confirmation, there were 830 candidates for that holy rite : and nothing could be more admirable than the order with which the whole was conducted. The vicar, in full canonicals, walked at the head of each file, as they approached the table, and his curate, also in full canonicals, headed each file as they returned to their seats. The effect was very striking, as we followed these shepherds with their little flocks, moving silently along the different aisles of that beautiful church ; while the good Bishop, as the representative of our Lord, stood with love in his heart, and blessings in his hands, to animate and encourage these followers of the Lamb, for their approaching encounter against the enemies of their salvation ! I am greatly in hopes that, of the ninety-nine whom I examined and recommended for Confirmation, almost, if not entirely, all will approach the Lord's table next Sunday ; and after having thus completed this blessed portion of my ministerial labours, which has occupied me for nearly two months. . . .

The fullest description of the practice of Confirmation since the Reformation is found in Canon Ollard's essay in the composite volume *Confirmation : I. Historical and Doctrinal* (S.P.C.K., 1926). There we read that " definite preparations for receiving Confirmation had ceased to be, in the later eighteenth century, a regular feature of the Church in England, and that candidates, at least of the educated classes, prepared themselves " (p. 212). " Bishop Wilberforce . . . was above all the remodeller of the practice of administering Confirmation, and the rite, which had reached the lowest depth of slovenliness and disorder in the early nineteenth century, was, owing chiefly to his practice, raised to a height of reverence and devotion which it had rarely, if ever, attained before within the period with which this essay is concerned " (p. 221).

Bishop Wilberforce was consecrated Bishop of Oxford in 1845. The passage from Anderson's Life quoted above shows that, in regard both to earnest preparation and reverent administration, great improvement had taken place, at least in some places, before the Tractarian Revival had had time to influence the Church.

XIII

MR. BROCKLEHURST OF LOWOOD

THE accuracy of Charlotte Brontë's memory of the school to which she went at the age of eight, as it appears in *Jane Eyre*, is obvious. The school is called Lowood, the clerical founder and superintendent Mr. Brocklehurst. The reader boils with indignation at the fictitious narrative, so clearly founded on fact. We need not dwell on the hardships, the bad food, and the unsympathetic treatment of the girls. Hardships were the lot of the poor, in which the children of the poor clergy had to share; many a school even today strikes a bad patch as regards food; and people in later life may well exaggerate the mental sufferings of a sensitive childhood. It is her Mr. Brocklehurst in whom we are interested.

He visits the school " buttoned up in a surtout and looking more rigid than ever ". He finds fault with details of the girls' clothes, with the extra food given once when the breakfast porridge was burnt, with the natural curls of certain children. Discipline, he says, is necessary. " Oh, madam, when you put bread and cheese, instead of burnt porridge, into these children's mouths, you may indeed feed their vile bodies, but you little think how you are starving their immortal souls ! " " Madam, I have a Master to serve whose Kingdom is not of this world : my mission is to mortify in these girls the lusts of the flesh." Jane Eyre in her nervous fright breaks a slate and Mr. Brocklehurst rebukes her. " You see she is yet young; you observe she possesses the ordinary form of childhood ; God has graciously given her the shape that he has given to all of us ; no signal deformity points her out as a marked character. Who would think that the Evil One had already found a servant and agent in her ? Yet such, I grieve to say, is the case." Was Evangelicalism ever so bad at this ?

These are the facts as given by Mrs. Gaskell in her *Life of Charlotte Brontë*. In July 1824 Maria and Elizabeth Brontë went to the newly founded Clergy Daughters School at Cowan Bridge, where Yorkshire, Westmorland and Lancashire meet ; Charlotte and Emily followed in September. The founder of the school, who kept the management in his own hands, was " a clergyman living near Kirkby Lonsdale, the Reverend William Carus Wilson ". He was one of twelve trustees, and himself treasurer and secretary, and devoted

135

much of his time to the superintendence of the school. The site had been badly chosen, he was badly served by the cook, a favourite against whom no one dared to inform, and the principles of sanitation were not understood. The result was an epidemic of typhus, from which Maria (Helen Burns of the story) and Elizabeth Brontë died. Mrs. Gaskell writes: " I need hardly say that Helen Burns is as exact a transcript of Maria Brontë as Charlotte's wonderful power of reproducing character could give." The same is true of " Miss Scatcherd ", whose real name is mercifully withheld. But what of Mr. Brocklehurst? Mrs. Gaskell regrets that, while one side of his character is faithfully represented, the delineation obliterates " nearly all that was noble or conscientious ". The early errors of management were eliminated and the later scholars used to speak of him with high appreciation.

But let Mr. Brocklehurst speak for himself. I have in my possession a little book called " *The Children's Friend* for the year 1828, by the Rev. W. Carus Wilson, M.A., Rector of Whittington, Vicar of Tunstall ". (Tunstall was the church, more than two miles away, which the children of Cowan Bridge attended, to hear Mr. Wilson preach. It was not warmed in winter, and they used to spend the time between the services in a chamber opening out of the galleries, where they ate a cold dinner.) The imprint is " Kirkby Lonsdale: Printed and sold by A. Foster ", to which the names of London booksellers are added. The volume is numbered V. Volumes I and II therefore were published in 1824 and 1825. We may assume that they were read by the children, including Charlotte, and that they were on the same lines as the fifth volume.

It is hard to imagine anything more unsuitable for children according to modern ideas. The January number begins with the massacre of St. Bartholomew's Day (five and a half pages). The next seven and a half pages describe the death of a little girl. " A true Account of the Punishment of Vice " follows, about a drunkard's death. Then another story of a little girl's death. Poems and hymns make up the rest of the twenty-four pages. In other numbers little children rebuke their parents and grandparents; small boys write pious diaries. Mr. Wilson in an article on " The Last Day " quotes a famous epitaph.

As I was travelling some years ago from Cheshire into Staffordshire, I stepped into the church-yard of a country village while the horses were changing. In walking among the tombs I met with this inscription, recording the death of a little child :

> When the archangel's trump shall sound,
>   And souls to bodies join,
> Many will wish their stay on earth
>   Had been as short as mine.

There is something delightful, and yet awful in these words.

He continues : " I would now address myself to the young readers of the Children's Friend . . . Every hour, you are advancing towards heaven or hell."

Elsewhere he quotes from one of his own sermons : " We cannot suppose, that you will *all* live to be men or women."

He tells the story of a little black boy who was brought to Sweden.

> He came once to a place where different persons were at dinner. At his opening the door, some of the female sex were frightened, on account of his black colour; but after hearing him speak, they could not but confess that he was a blessed youth. One of the company asked him which of the little ladies who were at the table he liked most. He replied, " I do not care for anything save the Word of God ".

Needless to say, he presently died.

It deserves to be noticed that the little magazine strikes a new note for those who have got their idea of children's literature from Mrs. Trimmer's and the other S.P.C.K. books, none of which lay this emphasis on the depravity of children or threaten them with hell. In justice to a good, if misguided, man we should remember that mortality among children was very great 120 years ago and a conscientious pastor might well feel it incumbent on him to prepare them for the possibility of death.

K

XIV

CHARLES DICKENS AND THE CHURCH

The Pickwick Papers appeared in 1836. According to G. M. Young (*Victorian England*), the work of the Evangelicals was done by 1830, and faith began to harden into a code. Up to about 1850, Evangelical observances strengthened their hold on the upper and middle classes, so that Dickens' first period of writing fell within a time of unchallenged Evangelical supremacy. Like most busy men, he probably relied for his prejudices on early impressions, so that we need not look for any development in his views about religion. He was born in a Church of England family, but his leanings were all humanitarian, and in 1843 he attached himself for a time to a Unitarian congregation.[1] The novels have no theological interest whatever, but they reflect popular ideas, and must in their turn have contributed largely to the reinforcement and propagation of these ideas. Intellectual difficulties seem to be non-existent. Religion, or rather religiosity, is presupposed as a vague background.

Before we look at the novels, we may ask whether Dickens' idea of the Church is not as inaccurate as his idea of cricket. In the famous description of Dingley Dell *v.* All-Muggleton, we are told that Dumkins and Podder scored fifty-four, and when their wickets had fallen Dingley Dell had scored 0. At an early stage in the game the latter gave in, without apparently batting at all. Dickens' caricatures of Dissenting ministers are probably no more trustworthy. But he views them entirely from the outside. He must have known something about so powerful an institution as the Church of England was then, and his testimony at least registers faithfully the popular verdict as regards things in general, though his details may be as inaccurate as his cricket lore.

David Copperfield's first impressions of Blunderstone Church have the photographic accuracy of a child's memories. The high-backed pew; the window through which Peggotty looked to be sure the house was not on fire; the sheep hesitating at the open door of the porch; the monumental tablets; the pulpit suggesting to him a boy playing "King of the Castle" and repelling another boy who comes up the stairs to attack; the preacher's velvet cushion with

[1] A. W. Ward, *Dickens*, p. 183.

tassels. Then, again, Canterbury Cathedral—" the earthy smell, the sunless air . . . the resounding of the organ through the black and white arched galleries and aisles " (chapter xviii). *Dombey and Son* has another vivid picture, of a town church this time, attended for a christening (chapter v), in which the light and air of Blunderstone have vanished. " So chill and earthy was the place. The tall shrouded pulpit and reading desk ; the dreary perspective of empty pews stretching away under the galleries, and empty benches mounting to the roof and lost in the shadow of the great grim organ ; the dusty matting and cold stone slabs ; the grisly free seats in the aisles ; and the damp corner by the bell-rope. . . ." By contrast, St. Clement Danes', where Mrs. Lirriper of *Christmas Stories* worshipped, is cheerful : " where I now have a sitting in a very pleasant pew with genteel company and my own hassock, and being partial to evening service not too crowded ".

In describing a country church Dickens could be farcical. Little Nell in *The Old Curiosity Shop* reached a village within sight of the Welsh mountains. " It was a very aged, ghostly place . . . and had once a convent or monastery attached." High up in the walls of the church were " small galleries, where the nuns had been wont to glide along—dimly seen in their dark dresses so far off—or to pause like gloomy shadows, listening to the prayers ". The church had a crypt, a dim and murky spot in which was a well, " dug at first (thought the sexton) to make the old place more gloomy, and the old monks more religious ".

English sentiment, says G. M. Young, clung to a picture of traditional village life with piously observed Sundays, " as Roman sentiment saw in the Sabine farm the home of virtue and national greatness ".[1] This helps to account for Dickens' idealization of the gentle white-haired country clergyman by contrast with the town parson whom he disliked. The " simple-hearted old gentleman, of a shrinking, subdued spirit ", who comforted little Nell is typical (*The Old Curiosity Shop*, chapter lii) ; he ministered to a flock of " humble folks ", many coming three or four miles to church. Tom Pinch, the organist of the village church in *Martin Chuzzlewit*, is a much loved figure. From chapter xxxi we learn that the organ was in a loft, and as the organist worked the bellows with his feet it evidently had no pedals. Mr. Pecksniff played the eavesdropper on Tom and Mary, hidden in a high red-curtained pew. When Tom had gone he sought the vestry, where he helped himself to port wine

[1] *Victorian England*, p. 21.

and biscuits and was startled by the appearance of two surplices, one black the other white, in a cupboard. When Oliver Twist reaches the country (chapter xxxii) he is taught by the clergyman, " a white-haired old gentleman . . . who spoke so kindly ". On Sunday " there was the little church . . . the sweet-smelling air stealing in at the low porch, and filling the homely building with its fragrance. The poor people were so neat and clean, and knelt so reverently in prayer." The clergyman of Dingley Dell in *Pickwick Papers* is sympathetically sketched. The whole party go to church on Christmas morning, and Bob Sawyer carves his name in letters four inches long (chapter xxviii). " The Convict's Return ", the tale told in chapter vi, refers to " the communion-table before which he had so often repeated the Commandments he had reverenced as a child, and forgotten as a man "—presumably the " Lord, have mercy . . ." of the ante-communion service is meant.[1] In *Reprinted Pieces* (" Sunday as it might be made ") Dickens speaks with high praise of the village parson who organizes cricket on Sunday evening, which may be a genuine reminiscence. But the Lincoln-shire village church in *Bleak House* " is mouldy ; the oaken pulpit breaks out into a cold sweat ; and there is a general smell and taste as of the ancient Dedlocks in their graves ".

We must not forget Traddles' father-in-law in *David Copperfield*, the curate in Devonshire, who had ten children, mostly girls, none of whom apparently works for her living. Traddles visits Devon-shire, walking there in eight days.[2] The best paid curates at this period were in the diocese of Rochester, according to G. M. Young (p. 63), where stipends reached £109 a year.

In contrast to the country clergy, the town, or rather suburban, curate in " Our Parish " (*Sketches by Boz*) is described as an effeminate person, fussed over by pious women. The poor people rise to bow and curtsey as the rich lady enters. *Little Dorrit* displays a real *animus* against the Church. The Church bell is maddening, the congregation scanty. Clennam passes the lighted " windows of a congregationless church ". The only well-worked parish is Milvey's in *Our Mutual Friend*. The ways of a cathedral in the pre-restora-tion era are depicted in *Edwin Drood*, with Durdles the stonemason tapping the walls for traces of " old 'uns ".

Were churches really empty in Dickens' London ? The bulk

---

[1] Possibly catechizing in the chancel before the afternoon service is meant.
[2] Compare Hipcroft in Hardy's *The Fiddler of the Reels*, who in 1847 walks from Wessex to London, " one of the last of the artisan class who used that now extinct method of travel ".

of the people according to him were not in the least Sabbatarian. The typical city man sits out in the garden reading a Sunday paper. The people in summer pour out to tea gardens and crowd the river Thames (*Sketches by Boz*, sketches ix and x). Many steamers ply, loaded with excursionists. Churches, indeed, are well filled, but with fashionable folk; the sermon lasts twelve minutes only. Provision shops are open in the middle of the day. At dusk, " the roads leading from the different places of suburban resort are crowded with people on their return home " (*Reprinted Pieces*, " Sunday as it is "). This description dates from 1836. Probably large sections of the population were as " unchurched " as they are to-day. Mr. Young (p. 64) thinks that more than half the population in 1851 " went somewhere ". He quotes Lord Shaftesbury as saying that only 2 per cent. of the great underworld went anywhere. The world described by Dickens is largely underworld and certainly the Church seems to play a negligible hand in its life. In 1851, again, there were said to be 70,000 communicants in the diocese of London, out of a population of 2,000,000, a slightly smaller proportion than in 1939. It is significant that the Holy Communion is not, I think, mentioned in the pages of Dickens. There is a reference to week-day services in *Bleak House*. Esther Summerson's godmother " was a good, good woman! She went to church three time every Sunday, and to morning prayers on Wednesdays and Fridays and to lectures whenever there were lectures; and never missed."

But the Church in his novels is always there, in the background. The church clocks are always striking. Weddings in gloomy city churches abound. The only intellectual difficulty I have been able to find mentioned is the often too optimistic phraseology of the burial service (*Our Mutual Friend*, chapter x). The presuppositions of Evangelicalism are not shaken, though its sometimes unlovely manifestations are satirized. The non-churchgoers of Dickens may forget God, but they do not doubt his existence.[1]

[1] This sketch was written before reading Mr. H. House's *The Dickens World* (1941), which contains a chapter on Religion. He points out that the reforming movement of 1815–32 was saturated with religion. The emphasis was on Christ's mercy and love for the poor. Dickens appealed to a large public ready for Christian sentiment without dogma. He was not interested in faith or theology or worship; for him virtue is the natural state of man, and sin is hardly mentioned. As for the deaths of Little Nell, Paul Dombey, and Jo, " it is significant that the strongest contemporary protests against their pathos came from the religious press " (p. 132).

XV

AN EVANGELICAL PROTEST

In 1837 five Essex incumbents—Hastings Robinson, D.D., Henry Budd, Guy Bryan, Charles Isaac Yorke, and Henry B. S. Harris—published a book of 118 pages entitled *Two Memorials: addressed to the General Meeting of the Society for Promoting Christian Knowledge, on the alleged corrupt Character of some of its Publications.* They were all members of the S.P.C.K., and they expressed a dissatisfaction which had been simmering for some years. In 1834 the Society had replied to memorials received from various District Committees, to the effect " that it is not disposed to yield to unreasonable objections, nor to give up those principles of sound doctrine which it has so long maintained ; and that it is most anxious to maintain unchanged the character of the Society ". This reply did not satisfy the objectors, who in the next year made two definite requests : (1) that Foxe's Book of Martyrs be republished by the Society, and (2) that the existing tracts be subjected to a thorough revision. On January 5th, 1836, the Secretary replied that the reissue of Foxe's book was considered inexpedient, and that the attention of the Committee was being given to tracts on Popery. On April 5th a General Meeting was held, the Archbishop of Canterbury (Howley) being in the chair, and the Bishops of London, Bangor, and Gloucester being also present. The Standing Committee reported that the Tract Committee declined to undertake the revision of old books and tracts ; they had therefore decided that the duty of carrying out such revision should revert to the Standing Committee, who however doubted " whether they shall be able to discharge [it] in such a manner as to obviate all objections, or to give universal satisfaction " (S.P.C.K. Annual Report for 1836).

The particular tract discussed was Bishop Wilson's *Short and Plain Instruction for the better Understanding of the Lord's Supper.* The Tract Committee declined to consider any change of wording. The Committee, which consisted of seven members, included Hugh James Rose of Hadleigh, at whose house a famous meeting was held in 1833. (He was also a member of the Foreign Literature Committee, as was Dr. Pusey.) The Archbishop of Canterbury and the Bishop of London were sufficiently interested in the matter to attend the meeting at which the Committee's decision was reported and by implication approved, for the Standing Committee clearly intended to do nothing. Anyhow, the five clergymen prepared their book, which was presently published.

After a reference to " the present renewed aggression of Popish principles upon us ", which presumably means *Tracts for the Times*, the writers launch their main attack. The circumstances of the time when the Society was founded account for the deficiencies of its publications. About 1690, so Bishop Burnet wrote in 1713, Tillotson (then Dean of St. Paul's), Patrick, Bishop of Chichester, and he planned a new Book of Homilies.

> In the six Sundays to Whitsuntide [said Burnet] the doctrine of justification was to be explained; and some expressions in the first book [of Homilies] that seemed to carry *Justification by faith only* to *a height that wanted some mitigation*, were to be well examined; and all that St. Paul had writ on that head, both to the Romans, and the Galatians, was to be explained, and reconciled to what James wrote on the same subject.

Some of the Homilies were written, " dry and unevangelical " in character. A typical example of error is a statement by Burnet, approved by Tillotson, that " a charitable man that has had much occasion given him to forbear and forgive others, *dares lay claim to mercy and pardon*, with much humble assurance ". " Such ", say the writers, " was the divinity provided for the Church of England, by the Divines in whom this Society originated. . . . The same erroneous style of doctrine has prevailed from the very origin of the Society to the present day." The Society has consistently refrained from promulgating Reformation doctrine ; its publications show a legal spirit throughout ; they have " impeded the progress of divine truth by an unhappy admixture of error ".

Two works published by the S.P.C.K. have had an especially large circulation, Nelson's *Festivals and Fasts*, and *The Whole Duty of Man*. These are subjected to a detailed criticism.

What are " Saints in the Church Militant ? " asks Nelson, and answers :

> Such who not only believe the doctrine of the Christian religion, but conform their whole life to the precepts of it; such who not only have a holy faith, but are purified thereby ; who have a sincere regard to God and another world in all their actions, and are constant and uniform in the discharge of their duty ; who abstain from all kind of evil, " perfecting holiness in the fear of God ".

Impossible ! say the memorialists ; such a man " is not the subject of mercy; he requires no Saviour". Other errors are shown in Nelson's teaching about fasting and repentance—"We must repent to make us capable of that pardon he hath purchased for us"—and in what he says about the possibility of conquering particular vices.

> What wonder if this Papist in spirit should hold doctrines expressly papistical, such as—the Saints praying for us, and Mary, the Mother of God?

The Whole Duty of Man is "a work built on the same false and unscriptural principles as the preceding one". "The scheme of salvation, interwoven throughout," is "essentially defective, unsound, and dangerous." A particularly harmful passage is:

> The third thing that Christ was to do for us, was to enable us, or give us strength to do what Christ requires of us . . . requiring of us only an honest and hearty endeavour to do what we are able, and where we fail, accepting of sincere repentance.

Members of the Society are asked "solemnly to pause, and to consider the awful condition in which the Society, as they apprehend, appears as a Society for Promoting Christian Knowledge".

Minor works on the Catalogue are next examined. For example, *First Steps to the Catechism* contains this Question and Answer:

> Q. What must we do that we may obtain God's forgiveness?
> A. We must be sorry for our sins, and leave them off, and pray to God to forgive us, for the sake of Jesus Christ.

That is to say, the child is taught to obtain salvation by works.

Another tract, with the "Popish" title *A Companion to the Altar*, refers to "strict preparation" with a view to being "accepted by God as worthy communicants". It contains the un-Evangelical prayer:

> Clothe me with the wedding-garment, even the graces of the Gospel, and then I am sure that I shall be a welcome guest at the table, when I shall come thither in the likeness of thy Son Jesus Christ, in whom thou art well pleased. . . .
> Therefore help me to supply in humility what I want in worthiness.

The memorialists are hard to please; the wedding-garment cannot mean good works here.

The whole book strikingly corroborates the conclusions of Chapter I above. It is documented by quotations from the Articles and the Homilies, which seem to teach different doctrine. If the premiss is granted, that these sixteenth century formulas are the doctrinal standards of Anglicanism, the writers have a strong case. But they prove too much. On their own showing, the whole doctrinal position of official Anglicanism since 1698 had been non-Evangelical. Evangelicalism in the second half of the eighteenth century was something radically new, an emphasizing of certain aspects of sixteenth century theology which so far had failed to influence the Church of England. The writers of the Memorial have no good word to say of the intervening generations. We willingly admit that they have a case. The official theology presupposed grace, but was in danger of neglecting it in practice and of merely inculcating good works. If Evangelicalism was an interloper, it was one whose coming was necessary to revive the largely dormant energies of the Church of England.

I leave this forgotten controversy with the reflection that the protest, with its bold appeal to New Testament theology, was more worthy of Evangelicalism than much of the later anti-Puseyite agitation.

XVI

ENGLISH CHURCH LIFE IN 1850

LATELY I opened the bound volumes of *The Ecclesiastical Gazette* for 1849–50 and to my surprise found them so interesting that I was led to make notes on their contents. The magazine was published monthly by Charles Cox, whose office was near the Strand. It was in a way better than anything we have today. The three columns of small print were filled with official news: Parliamentary debates reported in full when they affected the Church, detailed accounts of law suits and of the proceedings of Church Societies, missionary intelligence, clerical preferments aud marriages, and University events. All this was pedestrian enough. Whatever was significant has passed into the history books, and the Review scrupulously refrained from taking any line of its own in Church matters. But it was far ahead of its time in commercial enterprise. Copies were sent free to all beneficed clergy, 7000 in number (new parishes being excluded), and on the strength of this a remarkable number of advertisements were obtained. In one number twelve pages of small type are thus filled. In these pages and not in the news part lies the interest of the Review. We overhear the clergy of the day in their business negotiations and their controversies, and we realize the unconscious assumptions of their lives. The sale of advowsons occupies much space. The details are frankly shocking. Clergymen advertise for advowsons or next presentations, stating how much they are willing to give. The amount varies with the age of the incumbent. Sellers generally give his age. He is eighty-eight, ninety-one, in feeble health, incapable of any duty, etc. There are several agents. One declares he has many hundred benefices to sell. Another that he has many advowsons still for sale, " although near the close of the season ". Inducements are held out that half the purchase price may be held over until the death of the incumbent, or that interest will be paid on the whole amount until his death. The value of the livings is remarkable. A large proportion of them are from £1000 to £2000 a year. One prominent agency calls itself "The Church Association". But the prince of agents was Mr. Ancona, presumably a Jew. Here is one of his notices, describing a valuable advowson, " offering an unusually advantageous opportunity for purchase by any gentleman

146

desiring to combine his duty with a large income and first-rate establishment. The parsonage is a handsome modern mansion approached by a park lodge, and standing in beautifully timbered park land, tastefully laid out with shrubberies and pleasure-grounds. The population is small, and income nearly £2000 a year." The same agent has a client willing to pay up to £12,000 for a suitable advowson.

The conclusion is irresistible that when W. S. Gilbert wrote " The Reverend Simon Magus " in *The Bab Ballads* he was not caricaturing certain of the clergy.

> A rich advowson, highly prized,
> For private sale was advertised ;
> And many a parson made a bid ;
> The Reverend Simon Magus did.
>
> He sought the agents : " Agent, I
> Have come prepared at once to buy
> (If your demand is not too big)
> The Cure of Otium-cum-Digge."
>
> " Ah ! " said the agent, " *there's* a berth—
> The snuggest vicarage on earth ;
> No sort of duty (so I hear)
> And fifteen hundred pounds a year !
>
> " If on the price we should agree,
> The living soon will vacant be :
> The good incumbent's ninety-five,
> And cannot very long survive. . . ."

And so on, up to the final touch that the vendor is a Jew. There is no sign that advowsons are being bought to safeguard a particular version of Anglican teaching ; all is unblushing commercialism.

The advertisements of proprietary chapels read curiously today. A clergyman desires " to purchase a chapel in the West End of London ". A sixty-two years' lease of a chapel is offered, seating 1000 persons and producing £600 per annum if all seats are let ; the present rent is £150. " The Church Association " advertises : " Freehold Episcopal Chapel, with its appurtenances, to be sold, suited to an Episcopalian of rather High Church views. . . . Price £1800."

By the side of the rich incumbents were the poor curates. The lowest salary offered is £50 : " should the applications be numerous, some will necessarily be unanswered ". £80 seems a standard salary. A London curacy of £100 is offered. By the side of this

I notice a Second Assistant Master wanted for a public school, for £40 residence. Nearly every number, by the way, contains an advertisement of a nomination for Marlborough, a bargain, or being sold cheap. Books were more expensive than they are now. Single sermons are published at 1s. or a higher price; Lectures on the Catechism at 18s.; Tupper's *Proverbial Philosophy* at 7s. and upwards. One tailor proclaims that, since the usual price for a clergyman's suit of six guineas is too expensive for some, he has devised a five-guinea suit. The poor curate of Victorian novels was a reality, like the rich rector.

How did the poorer priests live at all? Often tuition saved them. Fashionable clerical coaches could ask as much as £200 a year for pupils. Some clergymen came down to £30 or £40. Curacy wanted, says one, " with a fair probability of obtaining pupils ". Girls were generally educated at home. Governesses offer the rudiments of Latin, German and Italian, besides French thoroughly taught. Indeed, Italian is frequently mentioned. One boarding school for girls tells us that it teaches everything " from the first solid and well-grounded basis to the elegant and accomplished superstructure ".

The lot of a Secretary to a Society was much better than that of a curate. An Organizing Secretary to the London Hibernian Society is offered £250.

The advertisements for curates throw a light on the views of those who framed them. Requirements are completely different from those of today. " Ritual " and " ceremonial " are unknown words and " Catholic " occurs once only. A few ask for daily service and observance of festivals, but the general tone is Low Church; Tractarianism is disowned sometimes. The commonest description is the equivalent of our " no extremes ", namely " opposed alike to Romanism and dissent ". The Archbishops occur several times as a standard of orthodoxy. " Testimonials of agreement with the views of the Primate indispensable ", says one vicar. Another, a patriotic Northerner, says : " Wanted an earnest and pious curate, whose doctrinal views are in accordance with those of the Archbishops of York and Canterbury ". Elsewhere we find " sentiments in accordance with those expressed in the writings of Simeon, Venn, and Scott, etc." ; Dr. Hook's doctrine of Baptismal Regeneration is wanted by one vicar ; another says " what admits of clear demonstration from Barrow's works will not be disapproved ". This would-be curate is cautious : " he assents . . . in so far as he

understands the subject to [the doctrine] of our Lord's personal
advent and millennial reign "; but this one was a firebrand—he will
observe all the laws of this Church " in all their length and breadth.
In doubtful cases he must always refer to the Bishop for guidance."
Was the applicant who wanted a curacy where he may have a chance
of " conforming to the liturgy " a simple soul or a humorist ?

A fair number of applicants for livings, and even for some curacies,
offer to contribute to the Church or School Building Fund if appointed, which reminds us of the very rapid increase of population
and the extent to which the clergy taxed themselves to provide
churches and schools. Minor matters of clerical interest are the
humble beginnings of the summer holiday exchange of work system ;
the Auto-Crematic Gown, devised to meet " the many complaints
of the clergy of their robe slipping down the back as they preach " ;
and the many advertisements of barrel organs, for use in church or
at family worship. These are described as if they were scientific
novelties. An organ with ten tunes costs £15.; one with thirty costs
£80. An enterprising firm has introduced an " index ", by which
the name of the tune may be ascertained before it is played. But
what is a " Seraphine for use in church, £18 " ? As in private duty
bound I welcome the advertisement of " Bacon's Family Hotel " :
" its quiet central situation and proximity to the offices of the
Society for Promoting Christian Knowledge render it particularly
adapted for gentlemen of the clerical profession ".

School teachers are as well represented as curates in these columns.
Elementary education was managed by the clergy, who used their
professional journal for getting teachers. A school house was provided for man and wife, who were responsible for the teaching,
helped by pupil teachers. A typical salary for the two is £45.
£40 with children's pence, reckoned to bring in £10-12, is another
typical offer. Portsea was big enough to have a separate girls'
school, the mistress (" headmistress " does not occur in these
advertisements) of which was paid £40. Applicants generally
claim to be proficient in psalmody ; one is proficient in " spade
agriculture ".

Proprietary articles, other than chapels, are few, but the firm of
Rowlands advertises regularly. " Ladies travelling, or enjoying the
Rural Ride, a Drive, or Aquatic Excursion, or while otherwise
exposed to the rays of the sun ", are advised to buy Kalydor, as
used by the Queen. Rowlands' Pearl Dentifrice was also used by her.
Rowlands' Macassar Oil was bought by the Royal Family. The

Queen's name is not mentioned, but the dates suggest that she prescribed it for the future Edward VII and thereby helped to promote the flourishing Victorian industry of manufacturing anti-macassars. Has any historian recorded what Queen Victoria put on her toothbrush?

XVII

MRS. EWING AND HER BOOKS

THE recent centenary of Mrs. Ewing will have led some people to re-read her works, the mid-Victorian calm of which is delightful to a war-stricken generation. But they are valuable to the student, because they reflect so faithfully the ideals of a pious middle-class household in those days which now seem so far off.

Juliana Horatia Gatty was born at Ecclesfield, Yorkshire, where her father was Rector, on August 3rd, 1841. In 1867 she married Major Ewing, composer of the tune to " Jerusalem the Golden " which bears his name, and went with her husband to Fredericton, New Brunswick, where she remained for two years. In 1869 they returned to England and were stationed at various military centres, including Aldershot, the scene of some of her stories. Owing to ill-health she was unable to follow her husband to Malta in 1879. She died in 1885.

Mrs. Eden's Life of her sister reveals how much in the books is autobiography. Nurse Bundle in *A Flatiron for a Farthing* is Mrs. Ewing's nurse. Madam Liberality in *A Great Emergency* unconsciously describes her. Ida in *Mrs. Overtheway's Remembrances* is herself as a child. Reka Dom in the same book is one of her houses. The sickness which clouds the life of her child-characters reflects her own ill-health. These characters, like the adults, are real people, who are idealized by the author, always ready to believe the best of her fellow-men. *Six to Sixteen* is valuable for our purpose, being based on her own education. But the death-bed scenes which are so common are all imaginary, Mrs. Ewing never having been at one. An example of the way in which she used her childhood experiences appears in *We and the World*, where the mother's recipe for a child's being afraid of the dark was to recite the *Benedicite*. Juliana's own choice as a child was the *Te Deum*.

Mrs. Gatty, the mother, must have been a remarkable woman. Not only did she educate her daughters in the way described in *Six to Sixteen*, but she founded *Aunt Judy's Magazine*, called after Juliana's nursery name, as a vehicle for publishing the stories which her daughter told to the other children. From her teaching Juliana derived her love of languages, of dogs (so frequently described in her books), and of flowers, seen especially in *Dandelion Clocks*.

Most of the magazine stories appeared later in book form. A re-reading of the books will affect different people in different ways. Most of us will fail to get up enthusiasm for *The Story of a Short Life*, about a boy living near a military camp, or *Jackanapes*, another little boy who loved soldiers and died. The full-length studies, on the other hand, like *Mrs. Overtheway's Remembrances*, *A Flatiron for a Farthing*, *We and the World* (in spite of a poor ending), and *Six to Sixteen*, can still be read with great pleasure. In the last book a schoolboy says : " It's just like a man's writing about the careless happiness of childhood, when he is either forgetting, or refuses to advert to, the toothache." Did boys talk like that seventy years ago ? I can well believe they did, in Ecclesfield Rectory An interesting example of our changed views of what is suitable for young children is *Melchior's Dream* (1862), a story of Father Time and Death told to a nurseryful of children, which seems rather dreadful to us, but is considered by Mrs. Eden to be her sister's best story.

We have three pictures of girls' education : a boarding school, a schoolroom under a governess, and home education under a mother. It is rather horrifying to find the girls at school getting up at 6 a.m. to work before breakfast (*Six to Sixteen*). So do five girls, aged six to twelve, in the schoolroom. They are continually occupied throughout the day ; " hours that were not nominally ' lesson times ' were given to preparing lessons for the next day " (*A Flatiron for a Farthing*). In the home education described in *Six to Sixteen*, Italian is studied with gusto, mainly for the love of Dante, with the help of " six elaborate commentaries ". In most of the books children are enthusiastic for natural history, taking their cue from their elders. A significant touch is the reference to the mother's speaking to her children, " taking her eye from the microscope " (*Six to Sixteen*).

There is a charming picture of life at Eton, where the boys sketch, keep pets, make botanical collections, read poetry (a boy gives his fag a copy of Young's *Night Thoughts*) and cook " unparalleled dishes " (*Flatiron*). This seemingly is not a lady novelist's flight of imagination, for it is borne out by other pictures of public schools before the era of almost unlimited athleticism, when there was a better educational use of leisure than has often been found in recent years. However, Mrs. Ewing was not satisfied : " the insolent and undisciplined egotism of young children nowadays was not often tolerated by the past generation " (*Flatiron*).

Lest we, like Mrs. Ewing, should sigh too much for the past, there are many references to bad health. So many of the children are fragile, headaches are frequent, and illness is a continually recurring *motif*. It was an age of closed windows and bad drains. Eleanor, the adventurous girl in *Six to Sixteen*, would steal out of bed in the dormitory and open the window. A boy goes to work in an office which smells horribly. " The defects of drainage were so radical that . . . half the premises, if not half the street, would have to be pulled down for any effectual remedy " (*We and the World*). Ida falls into a little brook and runs all the way home. She goes to bed at once but immediately falls ill for a long time. When she is up again, she is not allowed out, though the day is " provokingly fine " (*Mrs. Overtheway*). The little boy in *A Flatiron* contracted a fever, but a devoted nurse saved his life ; she " fed me every ten minutes ". Yet Mrs. Ewing was ahead of her time. She speaks of " women's crass ignorance of the laws of health " ; " this kind of delicate-mindedness (is apt) to bring delicacy of body in its train ".

The Church forms the background of most of the stories. Children begin to learn the Catechism at three. (Mrs. Ewing was publicly catechized at four.) " At the public catechising, which came once a year, and after the second lesson at evening prayer, the grown-up members of the congregation used to draw near to the end of their pews to see and hear how we acquitted ourselves " (*We and the World*). The first Sunday School treat of the district is described, in farmers' waggons to a neighbouring town (*Flatiron*). Sunday School was at 9.15. A charming reminiscence is found in *Daddy Darwin's Dovecot*. " Countrywomen take mint and southernwood to a long hot service, as fine ladies take smelling-bottles. . . . Though Phoebe did not suffer from ' fainty feelings ' like her mother, she and her little playmates took posies to Sunday school and refreshed their nerves in the stream of question and answer, and hair-oil and corduroy, with all the airs of their elders." Phoebe said : " My mother always says there's nothing like bergamot to take to church."

Light is thrown on popular religious ideas of the period by casual references to Sunday observance, thrift and self-discipline. There is a charming picture in *A Flatiron* of Polly and the boy, forbidden

L

to climb trees on Sunday, devising a Sunday climbing game, in which three successive boughs are the clerk's desk, the reading desk, and the pulpit. The mother in *We and the World*, who, when her boys quote the Bible on a week-day, says, " Hush ! hush ! hush ! You're not to do Sunday lessons on week-days. What terrible boys you are ! " must surely have been drawn from life. With her we may couple the schoolmistress who confiscates the Apocrypha (in *Six to Sixteen*).

The Vicar's daughter in *Daddy Darwin's Dovecot* is planning how to get a workhouse boy, who has gone to live with a small-holder, into the choir. The Vicar's everyday coat is to be given up and his Sunday one used for every day. Her charity bag is to pay the tailor's widow to adapt the coat for the boy. Her old boots are to be re-soled and go to the boy, and an old pair of trousers to be obtained from her cousin. It was the day of small things for many middle-class people, one to which we may have to return. Mrs. Ewing inculcates what seems to us an almost inhuman thrift. " A self-indulgent civilisation goads all classes to live beyond their means. . . . It is well to remove a due proportion of what one has beyond the reach of the ever-growing monster of extravagance " (*A Flatiron*). This is at a time when the rural labourer's wage was 9s. a week, according to the same book !

Evangelicals and Tractarians agreed in inculcating self-discipline. Even so, the assumption in the following quotation is surprising : " *like most conscientious girls*, we had rules and regulations of our own devising : private codes, generally kept in cipher, for our own personal self-discipline " (*Six to Sixteen*).

Class distinctions are naturally assumed. " Of course, I do not mean to say that as many ladies as servant-girls tell untruths " (*Six to Sixteen*). " Uneducated people and servants have not—as a class—strict ideas on absolute truthfulness and absolute trust-worthiness in all matters " (*A Flatiron*). And this dictum is illuminating : " Children, like other uneducated classes, enjoy domestic details " (*We and the World*). The ideal is a house run by servants, who set the mistress free for the things of the mind and the spirit. But the ordinary middle-class woman fell far short of the desired standard. " To talk on any subject beyond mere chit-chat, and be understood, was a luxury we did not often taste at the tea-parties of the town " (*Mrs. Overtheway*).

The reader will have formed his own conclusions by now. There has been no space in which to explain how much the picture of childhood drawn by Mrs. Ewing differs from that familiar from the novels of the post-Freudian period. Were children ever so innocent and sweet, and so determined to be good, as these children of hers ? If, as many old people will testify, they were, or at least the girls were, in many sheltered middle-class homes, educational " progress " has not been so marked as we should like to think.

XVIII

A FAMILY BUDGET: THE CRAWLEYS OF HOGGLESTOCK

THERE are few domestic economies so vividly portrayed in fiction as that of the Rev. Josiah Crawley, Perpetual Curate of Hogglestock in the Diocese of Barchester, who is immortalized by Anthony Trollope in *Framley Parsonage* (1861) and *The Last Chronicle of Barset* (1867). The poor half-cracked priest is the real hero of the Barsetshire Series. All I propose to do in this note is to examine his yearly budget and to suggest that, as you would expect, he was a bad manager.

He appears first in *Framley Parsonage*, where his early struggles as a curate in Cornwall are told retrospectively. He was at Oxford with Dr. Arabin, his lifelong friend, but in spite of his wonderful scholarship, of which we are assured, was left to languish on a stipend of £70 a year. Neither he nor his wife, whom he married soon after being ordained, had any private means, and the birth of the four children, two of whom died, plunged them into debt. Arabin helped them constantly and finally paid Crawley's debts, and presented him with the living of Hogglestock, worth £130 a year. There we first see the family. Two babies have been born at Hogglestock, and it consists of Grace (aged nine), Bob (aged six), and the two babies.

At this period food was "used in quantities which any artisan would have regarded as compatible only with semi-starvation".

The Last Chronicle of Barset begins with the supposed theft of £20 by Mr. Crawley, which was really a gift from Mrs. Arabin. Dr. Arabin, now Dean of Barchester, had given him £50 lately, to which the £20 was surreptitiously added.

Three children are alive. Grace, aged nineteen, is teaching at a school at Silverbridge, where she gets her keep and a salary which at least enables her to "look nice". Bob is at school at Marlborough, probably at that date receiving free education as a foundationer. Anyhow, the Dean takes responsibility for him and his clothes. Jane, aged sixteen, is at home.

A pitiable description is given of the Rectory. There seems to be one living-room, the daughter, when disturbed by a visitor, retiring to the kitchen. The carpet has been literally worn out, so that nothing remains. The tables are broken. Mrs. Crawley shows in

her face the traces of her poverty.   This afflicted family of three
people and a maid (it never occurs to them that two women might
do the housework) consume 3 lb. of meat a day at 9*d.* a lb., costing
over £40 a year.   Bread costs at least £25 a year, say 2*s.* 6*d.* a week
per head.   Mrs. Crawley had to put up with " the taunt of the poor
servant who wants her wages ", but the girl did not starve.

Now what was the family budget ?   We are told that clothes cost
£10 a head for five persons, but Grace must have clothed herself out
of her £3 a month, and that the Dean paid for Bob's clothes is
expressly stated.   Food has been already mentioned ; wages were
left unpaid.   But what came into the house ?   In the twelve months
preceding the alleged theft we know of the following, to say nothing
of frequent gifts in kind from Lady Lufton and others :

	£
Income of living	130
Value of house (say)	30
Given by Dean Arabin	50
Given by Mrs. Arabin	20
Sent home by Grace	6
Literary earnings	5
	£241

The last item refers to a payment by an " admiring magazine editor "
for a translation into Greek irregular verse of " the very noble ballad
of Lord Bateman ".   I know of no more poignant illustration of the
cultural darkness in which we now live in comparison with the light
of seventy-five years ago than that Trollope could have penned what
seems to us so ludicrous a sentence.   Now consider that rates and
taxes would be negligible, prices were much below those of today,
and that the onions used for the mutton broth, of which we read,
presumably came with much else from the garden, the Crawleys'
income from all sources was in the neighbourhood of £500 a year,
translating it into terms of 1938 ; perhaps £750 in those of 1944.

We must conclude that Trollope wrote in the light of his middle-
class comfort and did not criticize his own assumptions.   The statement that the food consumed by the Crawleys would have seemed
" semi-starvation " to an artisan is absurd.   A Wiltshire labourer
at that time was paid about 10*s.* a week.   Grace, again, who looked
" quite nice " at Miss Prettyman's school, and attracted Major
Grantly as a suitor, when invited to visit Lily Dale at Allington,

came home and spent weary hours in sewing " that she might not reach her friend's house in actual rags ". No, we cannot take Trollope as a reliable witness to the relative standards of living in his day. But the two items of food of which he gives exact figures are significant. Meat cost 9*d*. a lb. (they must have insisted on having prime cuts only, as prices were then), and they ate 3 lb. a day. And they ate 2*s*. 6*d*. worth of bread a week per head. I remember the 1*s*. 4*d*. 4 lb. loaf in the rationing period of 1918 just lasting out the week, for one person. By our standards the Crawleys had a badly proportioned dietary and enormously overate for sedentary people, so far as bread and meat went.

XIX

AN ILLUSTRATED PRAYER BOOK

A GEORGE I Prayer Book with portrait of the King, engraved title-page bearing the lettering " The Liturgy of the Church of England adorned with Sculptures ", and forty-nine engravings, is in my possession. The title-page bears the name of " Gucht " as the engraver. There is no clue to the date of the pictures, which may have been bound up with obsolete sheets of the Prayer Book. The date is 1727, and the book must have been printed in the few months before the King's death in June of that year. Bound up also with the Prayer Book are a devotional manual, *Companion to the Altar*, the title-page of which refers to the Act of Parliament of 1763, and the Metrical Psalter of Sternhold and Hopkins, dated 1725.

It was customary from the later part of the seventeenth century for dealers in prints to produce sets of engravings for binding up in Bibles, less commonly in Prayer Books. There was a considerable export trade in these, both from England and Holland. As no name is printed on the engravings of my book, the inference is that they are prior to the first Engraving Act of 1734, passed to protect Hogarth.

This paragraph is based on information kindly supplied by the Oxford and Cambridge University Presses.[1]

[1] The purpose of this note is to ask the reader to look at the pictures numbered 10 to 17, taken from the book. The Gunpowder Plot is evidently a popular *motif*. It also appears in the needlework of Dame Dorothy Selby (1572–1641), of Ightham, Kent, described by Mrs. Esdaile in *Country Life* of June 18th, 1943, where the eye of Providence casts a beam on which are inscribed the words " VIDEO RIDEO ".

INDEX

PRINTED AND BOUND IN GREAT BRITAIN BY RICHARD CLAY AND COMPANY, LTD.,
BUNGAY, SUFFOLK.

1. Marquis Du Quesne.

2. Lady Du Quesne.

4. William Jones.

3. Bishop George Horne.

Engraved by H. Meyer from a Painting by H. Howard.

5. Sarah Trimmer.

6. An S.P.C.K. Charity School.   Exterior.

7. Interior.

8. Badges worn by the " clothed " children.

Alphabet.

9. From Francis Fox's " Introduction to Spelling and Reading ".

Illustrated Prayer Book.
10. Descending into Egypt.

11. Lent I.

12. Trinity Sunday.

13. Trinity I.

14. St. Mark's Day.

15. Gunpowder Treason.

16. Martyrdom of King Charles I.

17. Restoration of King Charles II.